To Albert John

Happy reading

Gopal Dorai

# FROM VILAYUR TO BALTIMORE

A Lifelong Journey of Learning & Discovery

## GOPAL DORAI

Heritage Special Edition
**American Literary Press**
*Baltimore, Maryland*

# From Vilayur to Baltimore

Library of Congress
Cataloging-in-Publication Data
ISBN-13: 978-1-934696-09-5


Library of Congress Card Catalog Number:
2008901641


Published by

Heritage Special Edition
American Literary Press

8019 Belair Road, Suite 10
Baltimore, Maryland 21236

Manufactured in the United States

# Preface

My wife, Kamala, has been the driving force and inspiration behind this book. She has been prodding me for many years to write my life story. I kept putting off this project for a long time. Pressures of the academic life were foremost among the reasons. Of course one can find any number of excuses to avoid or procrastinate doing things that are not seemingly important or pressing. But a time comes when our priorities do change. What must be done suddenly takes precedence over other less-urgent tasks.

I finally started writing this book in November 2002. Many interruptions as well as unavoidable delays occurred along the way. Recording one's life is a challenging task, but ultimately rewarding.

Kamala urged me to record in detail as much of my childhood and village life as I could remember. I hope my children and grandchildren (and other readers, too) can learn much about that unique village environment in which I grew up. My childhood world, especially the rural, pastoral Vilayur I describe here, was very vibrant and real. That world is fast disappearing—indeed, it may already belong to a bygone era. The memories etched in my brain since childhood have been recorded here for the reader to visualize.

Part I of the book (INDIA) contains Chapters 1-12. It covers the period of my life in India, beginning with my early childhood, until my departure for the United States in 1963. Part II, (AMERICA) Chapters 13-24, deals with my professional life as a graduate student, teacher and as an immigrant in the United States.

Although I wrote this book at the urging of my wife, I do have other explanations for it. Why should anyone write an autobiography? Probably because the writer thinks that his or her life story is worth writing about. Ego has a lot to do with it. No doubt, the life stories of celebrities, statesmen, famous artists, writers, entertainers, entrepreneurs, actors and other well-known personalities are interesting. There is a lot of curiosity about the "rich and famous," as well as a perennial market for their life stories. Such memoirs have a ready audience, eager to read and learn about what the authors have to say.

Surely, I cannot claim any such prominence. I am just an ordinary guy. In my case, my motivation is somewhat modest. First and foremost, I want to convey to the reader a picture of my rural village life in Kerala of the 1940s. It was a colorful period. Very few people living today can recount such childhood experiences. My college education, too, was rather unusual. I have had some unique learning experiences. The circumstances of my marriage, though not uncommon, were full of challenge and intrigue. And my struggle to get a passport, my efforts to raise money to buy a plane ticket to the United States and the circumstances leading to the decision to become a U.S. citizen are noteworthy. I have tried to describe the early Indian immigrant experience of the 1980s, and its impact on both India and America. I was an integral part of that historical saga. Finally, I wanted to share with readers some of the wisdom and lessons I have learned through many interesting life experiences as well as a lot of reflection. I hope these may be relevant and useful to others in their journeys through life.

I dedicate this book to all my teachers. They made me who I am, and provided the impetus needed for me to study, work hard and live life to the fullest. Foremost among them was my father, who was my first teacher.

**Ellicott City, MD**

November 2007

## Acknowledgements

When I showed an earlier draft of this book to my brother, K.G. Ramakrishnan, he went through it carefully and methodically and suggested several improvements. So did my daughter, Vidya Ambrosi, who has a keen eye for style and substance. Without their valuable input, the book would not have been as readable as it is. V.N. Subramanian painstakingly brought to my attention many typographical errors, which I am glad to correct. Jon Berry spent several hours of his Thanksgiving holiday to format the book for the publisher. To him goes the credit for its beautiful layout. I am also happy to give my heartfelt thanks to Donna Wessel, Director of Publications of American Literary Press, for her timely assistance in bringing the book to fruition.

Finally, and most importantly, my grandchildren: Niklas, Kristofer, Aarthi, Anand and Anil certainly made all my effort in writing this book both enjoyable and worthwhile. I hope they will savor and recall with pleasure their grandfather's labor in writing his life story for their reading as well as for future generations.

# TABLE OF CONTENTS
## PART I: INDIA

## PART II: AMERICA

# Chapter 1

## Vilayur: Rhythm of Village Life

Perched between the Arabian Sea and the Western Ghats (also called the Sahyadri Mountains) in the southwestern part of India lies the state of Kerala. The word "Kerala" literally means "land of coconuts." This is a lush, evergreen, tropical paradise that the people of Kerala call "God's Own Country." The length and breadth of the land is dotted with coconut trees. The most important crop grown in Kerala is rice. Most of the people living there are farmers engaged in cultivating rice as well as many other commercial crops, such as rubber, coffee, tea and spices. It was in search of these celebrated oriental spices that the Portuguese sailor/explorer Vasco da Gama landed in Calicut, on the West Coast of Kerala, in 1498.

In recent years, Kerala has been attracting large contingents of Western tourists seeking relaxation, peace and tranquility. Its many quiet and beautiful beaches in Kovalam and elsewhere beckon fun-loving travelers from distant lands. Its one-of-a-kind wildlife sanctuary in the "Silent Valley" area in the Western Ghats has attracted the attention of conservationists worldwide. Those seeking the ancient ayurvedic health and beauty treatments (for a holistic lifestyle) can find their nirvana in rejuvenation centers throughout Kerala. Tourists from all over the world can also enjoy the unique floating boat holiday experience in the backwaters of Kerala's beautiful Vembanad Lake.

My birthplace, Vilayur, is a small rural village situated in the heart of Kerala. You probably will not be able to see it on a tourist map. To get there, you must first take a train to Pattambi, the nearest railway station, which lies on the rail route between Coimbatore (in Tamil Nadu) and Calicut (in northern Kerala). From Pattambi, buses ply to Perintalmanna, about twenty miles away. On this road, about seven miles from Pattambi, is the Vilayur post of-

1

fice. Once you reach this landmark, you have to walk toward Vilayur village. (Nowadays taxis are available; but until recently, walking was the only way to reach the village.) The walk takes you
through a narrow, winding, partly paved road, on both sides of
which there are scores of small houses, paddy fields, banana
groves, and lots of other greenery. After walking for about two
miles, you begin to see some thatched-roof huts, small stores, a
couple of tea stalls and a schoolyard on the left. This is the Vilayur
Primary School. Continuing your walk for another quarter mile or
so, you reach my ancestral house in the ancient village of Vilayur.
You are now at the place where the subject matter of this journey
begins. Welcome to Vilayur, the village that civilization forgot.

The year is 1947. Imagine: you are transported to a place that is
quite unlike anyplace you have seen before. It is early in the morning on an October day. The air around you is almost pure, and the
sky above is a clear azure blue. A gentle breeze wafts in the air.
Laden with heavy dew, the plants around you are bursting with
beautiful flowers. The sun slowly emerges in the distant eastern
horizon. All around you, as far as you can see, are green carpeted
rice fields. These are interspersed by small clusters of coconut and
palm trees, standing tall and majestic, shooting into the sky.

Bordering one of these tree banks is a beautiful small pond,
about two acres in size. Lilies and large-stemmed lotuses are floating on its surface. Some large bushes are to be seen on the far edge
of the pond. These bushes are adorned with crimson, yellow and
white flowers. White jasmine and other exotic tropical plants are
radiating their fragrances into the air. The plentiful dew on the
pepper vines is slowly turning into droplets of water as the rising
sun is slowly warming the air around. Scores of birds are chirping
from the trees all around you. Not to be left out, the frogs hiding in
the rice fields are croaking incessantly. An occasional bird is diving into the pond to look for an early breakfast of fish swimming
underneath the still waters.

With gentle, measured steps, some village women, carrying in-
fants in their arms, are walking through the rice fields. The fields
are divided by what looks like ribbons of very narrow walking

2

pathways, called varambu. This word literally means "border." These paths are generally no more than two feet wide. They are raised about six inches above the paddy fields. The varambu not only enable the villagers and cattle to walk through the otherwise water-soaked fields, but more importantly, help to divide the larger fields into identifiable smaller plots. Each plot or a group of plots may belong to a different farmer, cultivator or absentee landlord.

This typical morning village scenery does not seem to have changed for centuries. These people and the land they inhabit seem to blend together beautifully. Here and there are small homesteads tucked away behind a cluster of trees. Small bamboo fences demarcate the homesteads from one another. Such tiny hamlets are spread throughout the village, where the workers and their families live. There are some thatched roofs sticking out of the greenery that surrounds them. These are the homes of village farmers and artisans living in Vilayur. The farmer's children, his small cattle and other farm animals such as goats and hen wander around freely everywhere.

The topography of the land permits plenty of grazing land for the wandering animals. Behind the village is the large Chelambra Hill, part of the Sahyadri chain of mountains. The small hillocks and meadows surrounding this large hill are home to a few wild animals such as fox, deer, porcupine, peacock and many species of reptiles. The dense forest on the big hill is home to a tigress and its cubs. The villagers are constantly complaining about how their cattle are attacked by the marauding animal. They are afraid to leave their milking cows and calves in the meadows unattended for fear of the tigress.

Village life revolves around agriculture. Most of the residents are farmers. A few artisans such as carpenters, blacksmiths, potters and assorted other craftsmen eke out a living by catering to the villagers' needs. A couple of tea stalls and small stores selling simple household items (kerosene, sugar, cooking oil, salt, vegetables and tobacco) are the only shops in the village. The villagers seldom use cash. Most of their transactions are done through barter. On some evenings, the men folk congregate in the neighborhood arrack shops to drink their favorite liquor. This is a crude form of locally distilled beer, tapped from the palm trees. It is abundant and cheap. Here the men congregate, gossip, argue, and sometimes entertain themselves into a drunken stupor.

Agricultural work in the village is seasonal. There are two rice crops, mainly dependent on the monsoons. During the rainy season, the nearby river sometimes inundates the low-lying farmlands. Water is always plentiful in the village. Some farmers even manage to cultivate a third crop on portions of their fields near large wells. The fields are irrigated by time-tested ancient techniques that are labor-intensive. The perennial supply of dung from the animals and leaves from the household trees provide manure for the crops. Such ancient methods of farming have kept the environment healthy and clean. One can almost always see large numbers of farmers, both men and women, bent over their plots doing various chores: tilling, weeding, planting, picking and harvesting. The land and the people harmoniously blend with the environment.

For centuries, the people living here have been tradition-bound in all aspects of life. Modern technology and its methods are alien to them, and are seldom used. People are either unaware of them, or cannot afford to adopt them. Diseases are treated by using local herbs and ancient healing methods practiced by traditional "vaidyas" or medicine men. Antibiotics and modern medications have not been in use, if at all, until very recently. Young mothers give birth to their children in their own homes, sometimes assisted by older, experienced women or village midwives. Many of these young mothers die while giving childbirth. Infant mortality is relatively high even today.

When I was growing up in the 1940s in Vilayur, I used to hear many stories of animal sacrifices to placate the fiery Goddess Kali. The villagers were terrified when a case of smallpox broke out. Most of them believed that the fierce Goddess was responsible for this mishap. For some inexplicable reason, the Goddess had become angry, and she had to be appeased to ward off the disease. In order to placate Goddess Kali, it was necessary to sacrifice a goat or a hen. If the pox was cured, they believed that Kali was satisfied

4

by the gift of the animal's blood; if not, the Goddess was still angry with the afflicted person. Either way, the Goddess had great powers, and her blessing was needed to survive.

Many other ancient beliefs and superstitions dominated the villagers' thinking. Various types of demi-gods as well as ancient demons were worshipped in turn. Children were told that if they cried too much or misbehaved, the demons would become angry and punish them, or even eat them up. These demons were supposedly very powerful and active after nightfall, when they were thought to be prowling around the village, looking for prey. Some of the children were terrified to go outside the house in the dark. Rumor had it that the forests around Chelambra Hill were the favorite abode of these demons and demi-gods.

Although there was a primary school in the village, many parents did not bother to send their children to school. By the time children reached the age of eight or nine, their parents needed them on the farm. The economic value of a child, as a laborer, was high enough to dissuade most illiterate parents from sending their children to be educated. The illiteracy rate in Vilayur fifty years ago was probably around 95 percent. Most villagers did not know how to read or write. They did not seem to appreciate the value of education. Especially during the planting and harvesting seasons, it was handy to have plenty of child labor at home to do various chores. Therefore, parents did not want to send their kids to school. Thus the cycle of illiteracy and poverty was perpetuated for generations, until very recently. Most of the parents preferred to have large families. The general attitude was that a child not only comes into the world with one mouth, but also two hands!

Although Vilayur was an idyllic village in many ways, it was extremely backward by modern standards. No doubt there were a few educated people in the village. They were the elite and relatively well-to-do farmers, landlords, teachers and a couple of local government officials. You could count them on your fingers.

Lacking most of the amenities of modern life, such as newspapers, electricity, medical care, transport and communications, these well-educated folks did not want to stay in Vilayur for long. Some of them left the village as soon as they were able to. Needless to say, there were hardly any employment opportunities in the villages for the educated. The story of my own life's journey, *From Vilayur to Baltimore*, started that way. In the following pages, this book chronicles how that journey came about, step by step. It is, indeed, a fascinating story, full of many adventures and numerous challenges that tested me to the utmost.

# Chapter 2

## Early Childhood Memories

I was born on December 21, 1935. My father, S. Gopala-krishnan, and my mother, K.C. Meenakshi, had twelve children. I was their third child.

My earliest memory of my childhood is probably around age five or six, when I was living with my grandparents in Karinganad, another pastoral village near Vilayur. Karinganad village was picturesque in many ways. It too was full of paddy fields, coconut groves and lush with tropical vegetation. These included several varieties of mangoes, jackfruits, bananas, tapioca, cashews, pepper, pineapples and numerous kinds of vegetables and fruits. In the midst of this vegetation, almost invisible from outside, stood our nondescript house.

The main living quarters of my grandfather's family consisted of a modest farmhouse. This was surrounded by two thatched-roof outhouses. There were several cows and buffaloes in one of these outhouses. The other outhouse was used as storage space for grains and cattle feed.

My grandparents, whom we used to call Appa and Amma (rather than the usual words: Grandpa and Grandma), brought me up during my early childhood. At that time, my parents were living in Vilayur, about three miles away from Karinganad. I think this was probably because my parents had many young children to care for and could not keep all the youngsters together in their tiny Vilayur household. I suspect it may also have been due to eco-nomic reasons, as my father's income was inadequate to feed and clothe all their kids. Other than this, I really do not know the dy-namics of why I was living with my grandparents rather than with my parents. Perhaps my grandparents wanted to have one or two youngsters around them, in addition to the many adults who were living together as a joint family. My three uncles – Kunchanna,

7

Chinnanna and Kunchappa – were part of the joint household.

My earliest memory of life in my grandparents' house was when I was probably five years old. In those days, my older sister Thylam and I were the only children under our grandparents' care. Amma woke us up very early in the morning, and the first chore of the day was to accompany her to the cowshed, where she milked the cows to obtain the morning's supply of milk for making tea. Sister Thylam and I would intently watch Amma milking the cows. It was our job to hold the calves away by long ropes to prevent them from suckling the mother's milk. This was a challenging task for both of us, because the calves would eagerly pull us back while Amma was filling up the jugs with fresh, warm milk from the cow's udders. As soon as the milking was over, we would go to the nearby tank to wash ourselves. This was a large pond about 100 yards from the main house, where we would all take our baths to purify ourselves in the morning.

Very early in my life, my grandmother taught me how to swim. She would tie together two coconuts with husk, just wide enough to hold my stomach in between them, and float me in the pond while encouraging me to negotiate the water with my hands and legs. We all learned how to swim very quickly. It was sheer pleasure to wade in the water for hours at a time after diving from a steep cliff (probably about twenty-five feet high). We learned to stay under water for long periods of time, counting to see who could stay the longest without coming up to breathe. Swimming was great fun, which we enjoyed to the utmost.

My grandfather was deeply religious, and did his morning ablutions and prayers with great regularity. He would spend perhaps an hour or more uttering various mantras (prayers) and slokas (verses), and doing many Surya Namaskarams (prostrating on the ground while worshipping the Sun God). These recitations were verses from the ancient Rig Veda. They were hymns designed to give us mental strength, purity, and invoking the various Elements in Nature (as well as Hindu Deities) for their continued bounty and blessings. He would also recite the sacred Sanskrit verse called *Gayathri*, repeating it 108 times. This mantra was an invocation to

8

the Sun God, seeking wisdom and enlightenment. After these rituals, he would drink his tea and attend to the day's chores.

Grandfather was the patriarch of our big farming household. One of Appa's daily routines was to walk around the paddy fields with a long T-shaped implement, forcing the rice stalks to bend away from the narrow varambus dividing the fields. He would meticulously bend the rice stalks with the long T stick. Then he would push them into the fields, away from the walkways, so that people walking on the varambu could not trample on the long stalks full of rice kernels. My job was to follow behind him to make sure the few paddy stalks that he might have missed to wean away from the varambu with his T stick were properly forced to bend away from those paths and into the paddy fields. This would probably take an hour or so. I enjoyed watching the heavy dew in the fields melt away in the heat of the rising sun.

My sister Thylam was three years older than I was. Both of us attended the local primary school. We walked through the paddy fields and along rows of houses sandwiched between acres of lush green fields. I was in the first grade then, and don't remember school very well. I studied in Karinganad for only one year. The next year, Thylam and I were taken by my parents to Vilayur. We stayed there for the next six years until I was ready to attend high school in 1947.

Life in Vilayur was extremely hard for us throughout those years. Food was always scarce. Essential staples were all in short supply. This was the time of the Second World War. My father was the headmaster of the nearby higher elementary school in Rayiranellur, about two miles away from Vilayur. Thylam studied in that school, while I attended Vilayur Elementary School. Father was also the manager (administrator) of Vilayur Elementary School. He enrolled me in grade three there. I don't know why I skipped grade two. (Was I smart enough to skip a grade?) The school was about half a mile away from home. We were drilled into learning the multiplication tables, ranging from numbers two to sixteen. This was the basic training needed to do most of the simple mathematical calculations in our heads. We were also required to repeat and recite these math tables every day before supper. After spending three years in Vilayur Elementary School, I graduated from grade five in 1945.

The daily rhythm of life in our household was chaotic. Father had too many things to attend to. He was a farmer as well as a teacher and an administrator, all at once. He managed the farm, milked cows, fed the buffaloes, grew vegetables, did shopping for the family, taught students in his classes, and also managed his elementary school (which consumed a lot of his time and energy). In addition, he also did work as an informal village counselor. He was always busy, with little time to take care of us. Numerous villagers would visit our household almost every day, asking father for advice, with requests to write petitions to the government and seek his counsel on innumerable farming problems. Once in a while, someone would bring him a bag of vegetables or a few coconuts as compensation for his services. With his meager salary and a large family to feed, he found it very difficult to manage the family budget.

In those days, the material conditions of living in Vilayur were indeed harsh. All my brothers, aged two to ten, including myself, wore what is called a coombalai, made from the leaves of the areca nut tree, to cover our nudity. The leaves were made pliable by warming them slightly so that they would bend into shape around our groins. It was considered acceptable to wear this contraption and walk around the house, even when visitors were present. That was the custom in those days. I suppose our father's clothing expenses for the male children were kept to the minimum because of this conventional arrangement.

The children never had enough clothing to wear, even to go to school. At any given time, we had probably two pairs of shirts and trousers. This pair used to be washed over and over again until they were completely worn out. We walked barefoot everywhere. I vividly remember that the very first time I wore something under my feet was when I was about sixteen years old. New clothes were certainly a luxury, perhaps enjoyed once or twice a year, for Onam (which was the annual festival celebrating the new harvest season

10

in Kerala). Occasionally, we drank tea and coffee without milk and sugar. Many times, the crude, locally made sugar known as jaggery was substituted for real sugar.

The youngsters were almost always hungry, looking for something to eat. Food at home frequently seemed to be in short supply. Once in a while, we would wander into neighboring fields, plucking and eating tender cucumbers that were just sprouting out of their vine. Or we would look for bananas that were beginning to turn just ripe on the plant, though hardly fruity enough to be eaten. Sometimes I would dig out the tapioca tubers, which grew in a bunch. After picking out one or two tubers stealthily, I would eat them hurriedly and replant the stalk back into the soil so as to make it appear as if it had been untouched! My sister and I used to have a contest picking mangoes early in the morning. A lot of ripe mangoes would have fallen on the ground during the night. They were sweet and absolutely delicious. Sometimes we picked the still-ripening fruits of the cashew trees.

I can vividly remember those days of rationing and severe shortage of basic commodities such as rice, sugar, cloth and cooking oils. Our family faced continuous hardship because these items were quite expensive, and often unavailable. Family finances were in such poor shape that we often did without some of the basic necessities. Father's income was insufficient to buy even the family's minimal needs for food and clothing. Sometimes we would go to our grandfather's house in Karinganad to bring vegetables, coconuts and other eatables to help us provide the essential grocery items. Grandfather's household grew many fruits and vegetables because my uncles (Chinnanna and Kunchappa) were good farmers. The main problem, however, was to carry the load on our heads or shoulders, and walk the three-mile distance back from Karinganad to Vilayur. That was an exhausting journey. I, Thylam and sometimes our father would bring as much stuff as we could carry on our backs. The path between the two villages was narrow, winding and at times treacherous. During the monsoon season, we would often slip and fall, spilling the contents of the sacks on the slippery wet ground. Even during the dry season, it was quite a

11

challenge to negotiate those narrow walkways, full of bamboo thorns and sharp-edged rocks. We had to dodge the thorns and rocks as best as we could. The experience of those difficult walks of my childhood is deeply etched in my memory.

The U.S. government used to provide milk powder and ground cornmeal under the PL 480 program to schoolchildren in Kerala during the war years. This was a perennial source of food in our household. Since father was the manager of our local school, he could divert some portion of the supplies for our own personal needs. This was a great boon during those days of acute food shortage. For almost two years, we grew up on American milk powder. It tasted funny compared to our own cow's milk—which was not always available when we needed it. The cornmeal powder was one of the basic staples used for cooking our "upuma" for lunch. We used to eat it day after day as a substitute for rice and other local kernels.

\* \* \*

NOTE: I guess it is the memory of those hungry, starving days that still haunts me when I see food being wasted or thrown away. To some extent, we do become victims of our own pasts, especially the most unpleasant experiences of our lives. Perhaps this explains why people who have gone through the dog days of the Great Depression admonish youngsters to cut down their spending and save money for a rainy day!

\* \* \*

As for recreation and entertainment, we were almost always self-sufficient. Most of the time, unsupervised by adults, the kids were left to entertain themselves or roam around the neighborhood as they pleased. We used to play hide and seek, skip and jump, draw large circles and squares on the ground, or play assorted games with neighbors. Our mother was always inside the house tending to her household chores. She had no idea what we were up to. When we got tired of these games and other antics, we started reciting poems that we made up, and sang songs. Or we challenged each other to repeat the multiplication tables, eagerly looking for each other's mistakes! The game consisted of reciting the multiplication tables without making a mistake.

Very early in life, Thylam and I were assigned several household chores. My job was to fetch water from the well, which was about fifty yards from the kitchen. The rope we used to fetch the water up from the bottom of the well used to break often. Consequently, the vessel tied to the end of the feeble rope would fall into the bottom of the well. Then our father had to spend several hours searching for a long bamboo pole to retrieve the vessel. He did not always succeed in this endeavor. Sometimes, the submerged vessel could not be retrieved, no matter how long and hard he tried. Then, a replacement vessel would have to be used to fetch the water. This often turned out to be an old, rickety, leaky bucket.

The problem was that the rope being used to pull up the bucket of water was often worn out and weakened from constant use. Almost always, it snapped back and broke while pulling up the water from the well. Replacing the old, broken rope with a sturdy, new one was probably an expensive proposition. Therefore, my father used to try to patch up the broken rope many times. Several small sections of the rope were tied together, forming innumerable knots, which constituted weak points in the chain. I guess money was so tight in the family budget that buying a new rope and /or replacing the leaky bucket with a new one was one of the lowest priorities in the general scheme of things—a costly alternative—which he could ill afford.

This whole episode reminds me of the story of the "Leaky Bucket." It illustrates how a lot of effort is often wasted with nothing to show for it. In many villages in Central Africa, water is a very scarce resource. The women have to walk a long distance to the nearest water source to collect water and haul it to their huts. This job takes up a significant amount of their time and energy. Unfortunately, the old, heavily used buckets in which they collect the water have tiny holes, and a lot of water leaks out between the time the buckets are filled at the wellhead and brought to their homes. The women may find that sometimes half the bucket has leaked out by the time they reach home. Yet they never bother to plug the leaks or buy new containers to collect the water, perhaps because they cannot afford to do so.

It is also well known that public spending by many welfare or government agencies to alleviate poverty has a similar "leaky bucket" syndrome. One dollar of expenditure borne by the tax-payer generally results in only half a dollar of benefit to the poor families who are supposed to receive such aid. This is because the administrative costs of running such a redistributive program are often high, and frequently absorb a high percentage of the money being distributed. Thus water as well as money often leaks out in the process of being collected and distributed.

One of the other tasks assigned to me was to take our cattle to pasture in the meadows. We usually had two buffaloes (used for plowing the fields), a cow (for providing milk) and a calf. There were several small hillocks and meadows around the village, thick with grass and other vegetation where the animals could graze and feed leisurely. My job was to lead the cattle about a mile and half away from our house through the countryside, making sure that they did not wander into the neighboring fields growing rice and vegetables. If the cattle inadvertently wandered into the rice fields or areas where crops were being grown, that would have enraged the farmers, resulting in quarrels and complaints (not to speak of crop losses).

After leaving the cattle to graze in the hillocks, I would return home to get ready to go to school. During the years 1945 to '47, I attended Rayiranellur Higher Elementary School, where father was the headmaster. This was the nearest middle school. The school was about two miles from our home. Many children from the Vila-yur area were studying there, including my sister Thylam. The path to the school meandered through picturesque paddy fields, crossing small rivulets and several homesteads that dotted the landscape. It took us about forty minutes to negotiate these walkways through prime agricultural lands. Often we carried our lunch in a small metal box. Many a time, father would ask me to accompany him to the teashop where he had lunch with his fellow teachers. He would buy me three or four small bananas for dessert after lunch. This

14

was a special treat for me. They were delicious, nourishing and very satisfying.

I studied at Rayiranellur for three years, which were my sixth, seventh and eighth grades. Father taught English in the eighth grade. He was a dedicated teacher as well as a hard taskmaster. He was known as a strict disciplinarian, and was often short-tempered. He got very angry if his instructions were not obeyed to the letter. Students used to be afraid of him. We were especially scared he would inflict physical punishment for not attending to our studies. In my school days, teachers had absolute control and authority over students. Those who did not do their homework or follow the teacher's orders were often subjected to flogging. This took the form of taking a "chooral" (cane or stick) with which the teacher would hit the student's extended palm three or four times. Sometimes the pain would be unbearable. There were times when I too was subjected to such beating. This fear of punishment instilled in me the desire to do my best. In retrospect, though, I think that genuine respect for father's good advice, and fear of his temper, encouraged me to do well in school as well as in other areas of work assigned to me.

My sister preceded me in each grade by a couple of years. She was not very studious, and failed in the final exam in the eighth grade. As a result, she did not continue her education beyond eighth grade. Although we belonged to a "progressive, educated family," I guess Father thought it unnecessary for a girl to be educated beyond the eighth grade. He was probably unwilling or unable to incur the expenses necessary to educate my sister any further. So she stayed at home after her eighth grade doing household chores—cleaning, washing, cooking and helping mother for a year or two. Then she went to stay with our grandparents, until she got married in 1954.

In addition to grade school education, this formative period of my early childhood, between ages five and twelve, also provided us with many rich cultural experiences. They were noteworthy, memorable and colorful. I describe them in the following chapter.

15

# Chapter 3

## Cultural and Religious Traditions

Throughout my childhood and adolescent years, we experienced the rich cultural life of the Kerala countryside. There were innumerable holidays and festivals throughout the year. The various holidays commemorated or celebrated many ancient myths and legends of the land. Several of the Gods and Goddesses were worshipped by rotation: Ganesha, Durga, Krishna, Rama, Bhagawati, Hanuman, Shiva, Saraswati and many lesser deities of the Hindu Pantheon. They each had their own important holidays, with different rituals, poojas, feasts, dances and festivities. The beginning of the monsoon season, heralding the arrival of the eagerly anticipated rains, started these festival cycles.

Vishu, the first of these annual holidays, symbolized the beginning of the New Year in Kerala. We would get up early in the morning and sit with closed eyes in front of the effigies of the various Gods. We were not supposed to open our eyes until the elders presented us with half-rupee coins and other small gifts to usher in the New Year. We had a specially prepared feast for lunch. This consisted of different types of rice preparations, several kinds of delicious vegetable dishes, plus fried *pappadams*. These were very thin, big, round wafers made from urad dal (lentils) and fried in coconut oil. It was a treat generally reserved for occasions such as birthdays and big holidays. A special kind of rice pudding, known as payasam, rich with sugar and ghee, would follow as the day's special dessert.

Then there was "Saraswati Pooja"—the start of the academic year. The picture of the Goddess of Learning (Saraswati) was placed prominently among several books and other musical instruments. The Goddess was worshipped with great reverence. Many flowers and garlands were offered to her. The blessings of the Goddess were needed to help us learn and become proficient in

17

our studies, music and the arts. This would also be the day of initiation of a young child to the world of writing and reading (and all forms of arts as well). Appa or Amma would keep us on their laps in front of the Goddess. Holding a chalk or pencil in our right hands, we would be shown how to start scribbling letters of the alphabet. The elders would then read stories from a book, or ask the older children to read aloud, so that the whole family could listen. Sometimes, white sand (or rice powder) was spread on the floor and children were made to write with their fingers on it. The children enjoyed the whole process of being introduced to the world of knowledge. It was considered both auspicious and significant in the youngster's life.

"Onam" was the greatest and most memorable festival season, celebrating the first big harvest of the year. The children would gather different kinds of bright flowers and make several circles, squares and other myriad geometrical patterns with them. These would adorn the courtyard in front of the house. It was indeed very colorful and pretty to look at. Big bunches of plantains, almost ripe but not yet ready to be eaten, were hung all over the house from the ceiling. This was the preferred way of storing them until they became fully ripe for consumption. The "Onam Day" was a memorable occasion, with different delicacies to feast upon. The culmination of the feast was pieces of baked plantain, ripe, delicious and filling. Everyone would get some new clothing as a gift from the family patriarch: either grandfather (when he was alive), or a senior member of the family.

The most interesting and memorable part of the "Onam" festival was the "Pootham Kali" (a demon dance). This dance was performed by a bunch of actors and players wearing elaborate tribal costumes. They would go from house to house during the season and enact various legendary events/stories from the Indian epics. Their foremost method of enacting these stories was through elaborate dances, intricate bodily movements, mimicry and various other contortions and facial expressions. These Poothams represented different demons, gods and goddesses. They would swirl and twist their costume-laden bodies rapidly, shaking their heads,

18

waving their hands and circling around for a few minutes. The purpose of these pranks was to enact the story and entertain the audience, consisting mostly of children from the neighborhood (though adults also enjoyed the show). Accompanying the troupe of dancers were drummers and singers with ancient musical instruments. Several hordes of these Poothams visited the village households during the course of the day. They would be given donations of rice and/or money for their performances. The festival period lasted for seven to ten days during the two harvest seasons of the year.

An interesting aspect of the Pootham Kali was its psychological impact on some children. In order to instill some fear among naughty and mischievous kids, the elder members of the family would jokingly ask the poothams whether they would take away such "difficult" kids, The poothams would nod their heads in the affirmative, signifying their willingness to oblige. Such trickery was sometimes employed for fun as well as to discipline recalcitrant children. It worked wonders on the youngsters!

Several other memorable cultural and religious festivals took place throughout the year. These were happy occasions for celebration, feasts and extended family gatherings. Each one followed the other in quick succession. Many of these functions were centered on the local temples, of which there were so many in every corner of Kerala's countryside. The Annual "Thalapoli" or "AARAT" was the biggest of these temple events. Honoring the deity of the local temple was the guiding spirit behind these celebrations. The village elders would make elaborate preparations for the event. The villagers would eagerly await the festival, which was full of pomp, great spectacle and endless entertainment.

The highlight of the festival was the big elephant procession. Several elephants, specially brought for the occasion from other larger temples (which could afford to keep these elephants in the normal course of their operations), were beautifully decorated with colorful costumes from head to foot. These caparisoned elephants, along with a whole retinue of drummers, pipers, musicians, dancers and hundreds of young women carrying lighted lamps, would start the procession from the front of the temple.

The procession would march slowly and deliberately forward to the village center for several hours, with the various groups of drummers, pipers, musicians and dancers taking their turns to display their wonderful skills in front of the enthralled audience. The sea of people around the procession would shout with joy. Encouraged by the applause of the appreciative crowd, the drummers and dancers would vie with one another to excel in the display of their respective crafts. For hours on end, the delightful show would continue, entertaining everyone around. It was such a joy to watch, and all of us would eagerly wait for the next colorful event around the corner. From a distance, thunderous fireworks could be heard and seen, especially as the nightlong show drew to a close.

Religion dominated all aspects of our daily village life. The local customs and traditions were almost completely immersed in it. Ample tribute was paid to the many Gods and Goddesses of our legends by holding special *poojas* or celebrations in their honor. These deities were separately enshrined in different temples throughout the land. Each one of these temples had special significance in its own way. People would make pilgrimages to a particular temple to placate a particulate God or Goddess for different reasons: to relieve them from a certain bodily affliction, to beget progeny, to obtain success in a business venture, to offer thanks for winning a game, a civil lawsuit, and so on.

This temple-centric and religious orientation of life during my formative years made a deep impression on my young psyche. We were subjected to various types of superstitious customs, beliefs and modes of conduct, without any rational explanation of why we were following them. We simply had to follow the instructions of the elders. Questioning their knowledge or authority was alien to our nature. No one dared challenge them, even when they were probably mistaken. Fear and respect for the elders was inculcated in the minds of youngsters at a tender age. The overriding principle of family relations was respect and complete obedience to the elders. The central tenet of the elder-younger relationship was unquestioned subservience to authority or deference to age. We were

20

completely and thoroughly indoctrinated by many of the prevailing ancient customs of Kerala's rural village life. This may indeed be true throughout other parts of India as well.

Growing up in this atmosphere, I was steeped in many ancient religious traditions. I began to believe that my life—past, present and future—depended on the mercy of the local Goddess whom we worshipped, and who was the patron deity of our family. (Indeed, each person or family could have their own "Ishtadevata"— literally meaning favorite patron deity—who, above all other earthly powers would protect us from harm.) I accompanied the family elders on various temple pilgrimages. Fear of God(dess) — rather than love of God—gripped my mind. For a long time, I used to believe that my success in examinations or other personal ventures depended on the blessings and favors of the patron Goddess, rather than my own efforts. No matter how hard I worked toward my goals, if the Goddess was not pleased with me, I was sure to fail. I made promises to the Goddess that if she helped me to reach my cherished goals, I would offer her a special gift of thanks (donating a garland or a small amount of money to the temple). I did not realize until much later that such thinking, practices and customs were irrational and illogical. I was still an innocent lad of perhaps eleven or twelve years of age, and a product of my upbringing and environment.

One of these ancient customs, rigidly followed by my loving grandparents, was *untouchability*. During the middle 1940s, when I was barely ten years old, my grandparents were staunch believers in the doctrine of untouchability. Whenever we came anywhere near the vicinity of the various castes of untouchables—who were employed by the upper castes (classes) to do all the dirty and menial jobs (tilling the soil, weeding, seeding, watering, harvesting, husking and collecting the grain from the fields)—we had to keep our assigned distance from them. We were supposed to observe the custom meticulously. If, perchance, heaven forbid, we came closer than the sanctioned or prescribed distance within the untouchable person's physical proximity, we had to run and take a plunge (bath) in the "kolam" (water tank or pond) before we entered the house. The distance—measured in feet—required to be kept between us (Brahmins) and the untouchables (before we could be pronounced "polluted") was dependent on the particular tribe to which the untouchable person belonged. There were different categories of untouchable people, some much more untouchable than the others! It was all a matter of caste hierarchy. To a large extent, this depended on how menial and unpleasant, or dirty, their particular profession was.

We knew who the untouchables were by their surnames and their tribal affiliations. We were trained to mentally measure the approximate distance we had to keep between their physical location and ourselves. They were required by custom to shout some distinct sounds or syllables loudly from a distance, signaling their proximity and whereabouts. Hearing their sounds, we would avoid going near them. They were trained, much as we were, to keep the requisite distance from us so that we would not become polluted by their presence. As I said, the prescribed distance was a function of the caste to which a particular untouchable person belonged. Everybody knew what the rules were. This idea of being polluted by going anywhere near the untouchable tribes was so ingrained in our young minds that transgressing the dictum would bother our consciences, even if the elders were not around to watch or supervise our behavior. The indoctrination was thus total and complete! So, if we had to go near them for any reason, or by sheer accident, we would automatically acknowledge that we were being polluted, and would proceed to take our bath before entering the house. Such was the power of custom and ingrained habits!

I tried to describe this ancient custom in some detail because one of the heretic acts that I did was to challenge the notion of getting polluted by going near the untouchables. I still don't know, nor can I explain, what came into my mind, and why I did what I did. One day, I confronted my grandfather and asked him, probably in all innocence: "Appa, what is 'ayithom?'" (This is the Malayalam word for the doctrine of untouchability.) "Can I see it and touch it?" Such a question was pure heresy, an unthinkable act of disobedience on my part. My words, nay, my question, infuriated my grandfather so much that he started chasing me angrily

22

my grandfather so much that he started chasing me angrily and shouted at me, eager to punish me for my impertinence. I ran fast to avoid being caught by him, and the chase continued for a while. No doubt, I ran much faster than my grandfather, and he eventually gave up the chase, but declared: "When I get you again, I will deal with you properly." I suppose my grandfather was completely shocked, dismayed, taken aback, by my uncharacteristic behavior and remarks. I suspect he must have been at a loss for any rational explanation of the concept of ayithom, probably due to his own unflinching and deep convictions, inherited from his ancestors. The episode was soon forgotten—neither of us discussed the subject ever again. Afterwards, I was contrite and felt rotten for questioning his wisdom and authority. The incident tore my heart for a very long time afterward. I really did not mean to hurt my beloved grandfather's feelings.

During those formative years of my life, I used to frequently accompany my grandfather or my uncle Chinnanna to various temples. We would sometimes walk four or five miles at a time to go to these temples. The temples were always preparing large feasts during the various religious functions or Hindu holidays. Appa and Chinnanna were well versed in cooking, and the organizers of these feasts used to recruit them to prepare food in the temple kitchens. They were able to earn some cash income for their labors. (I use the term "cash income" deliberately because my grandfather's family was a self-supporting subsistence farm family with very limited marketable surplus of grains. The major source of revenue (cash) was from the occasional sale of small quantities of commercial crops such as pepper, tapioca, coconuts and some rice. I suppose the cash income generated by these sales helped to finance the purchase of the grocery items needed for running the household.)

I remember vividly the excellent food we enjoyed at these temple feasts. Sometimes my uncle would take my elder brother Mani as well as myself along with him. The ancient Brahmin culture of Kerala was such that we could simply walk into any of these public temple feasts, almost always unannounced, and not have to worry

23

about money to buy food. A Brahmin boy such as me (who wore a sacred thread on my chest visible for all to see, an insignia of Brahmin boys) could easily survive on the temple premises, getting free food and lodging without any questions being asked. The temples were very generous public institutions, financed by well-to-do upper-class families or religious endowment trusts. If one were even slightly religiously oriented, one could make a modest living by hanging around the temples and doing some minor chores (such as collecting flowers, making garlands or doing some cooking). In fact, our family frequently participated in these activities as a matter of course.

The Kerala of my boyhood has undergone rapid change. At that time, the economy of the land was very primitive and pastoral. Cash transactions were minimal. We used to pay our workers (occasional hired help) in food grains: their daily wages, measured in containers of rice, were poured into a receptacle, which the laborers would haul away at the end of the day. There were very few roads linking the villages; we walked everywhere with our bare feet through the paddy fields or rocky pathways. We did not have many of the appurtenances of modern life such as radios, newspapers or even school supplies like writing paper and pencils. We grew up with slate boards and chalk to do our homework. We had no toys, but entertained ourselves by improvising games and playing outdoors. We did not travel much, except to visit the neighboring villages and temples, looking for country fairs and free cultural events. Life was, in many ways, unhurried and simple. Our lifestyle was characterized by a perennial absence of cash transactions—the village economy was almost self-sufficient for our limited needs. Barter was prevalent everywhere. I did not know what the outside world was like, because there was hardly any exposure to the world beyond our own villages.

In those days, most of the village folk never traveled more than twenty or thirty miles during their entire lives. There was indeed no reason to do so. Life was very simple, and one's material wants were few. The average annual income of a typical rural Kerala family in 1950 was about 250 Indian rupees. In terms of purchasing power, this was probably roughly equal to $150 at that time—roughly half a dollar per day. It was just barely sufficient to eke out a limited existence, even by village India's standards. Income and price levels have changed many-fold in the last fifty-plus years. In terms of 2007 purchasing power, this would probably represent roughly 2,500 rupees, or about $400 (this estimate is not based on any official exchange rate, but an approximate reckoning of rural living standards).

\* \* \*

NOTE: Throughout this book, I have used local currency figures, without any price adjustments, as and when the events described herein took place. The Indian rupee was valued at about Rs.4.89 to the U.S. dollar in 1950. There have been many exchange rate adjustments during the last six decades. The exchange rate in 2007 is about Rs.42 per U.S. dollar. Prices of various commodities and services in India and USA differ markedly due to a number of factors. The consumption patterns in the two countries are vastly different. The prices of many goods and services purchased by the typical American family are not included in the Indian (Kerala) villager's consumption basket. To do so would distort international comparisons beyond credibility.

\* \* \*

The old patterns of living have changed now, of course. When I visited my native village in 2006, the place had been transformed beyond belief. Paved roads, hundreds of motor vehicles, scooters, bicycles and bustling traffic have changed the landscape as well as the old ways of life. No one walks much these days, especially the youngsters. Rural electrification has brought TV and radio into many households—not everyone can afford them yet. TV sets, cell phones, blaring loudspeakers, Internet cafés, and well-dressed crowds are seen everywhere. Many new movie theatres, schools and even junior colleges have sprung up throughout the land. Untouchability is a distant memory; it has been outlawed. Signs of economic progress abound in Vilayur.

The meadows and fields where I used to take our cattle to pasture have been transformed into large plantations of rubber, coffee and many other commercial crops. The hillsides have been denuded of trees, and new housing for the growing population has replaced many old farms. Signs of urbanization have crept into those villages of yore.

* * *

Before I conclude this chapter and proceed to describe my high school education in the next, let me recount two other events that brought me into contact with modern civilization and urban life in my early boyhood.

The first of these was a railroad journey to attend the marriage of my maternal uncle, Mr. Krishnamurti, in Trichy, one of the largest cities in Tamil Nadu, about 300 miles from Vilayur. In order to get to the railway station in Pattambi, which was about seven miles from our home, we had to first travel by a bullock cart. Perhaps my mother was pregnant at that time. There were other young children (my younger brother and baby sister) who could not walk the entire long distance to Pattambi. Therefore, after walking for about two miles to reach the paved road in Rayiranellur, my father had engaged a bullock cart to take us to Pattambi. That was a memorable journey in itself.

We started from home after dinner. After walking for about an hour or so to reach Rayiranellur, we boarded the bullock cart. This road was not very well paved. All of us—parents and children—huddled together into the inhospitable and ramshackle cart, and squatted inside. For about two or three hours, the slow-moving bullock cart pulled us through the dark night toward Pattambi, probably at a speed of about two miles an hour. We were all so excited about the forthcoming rail journey that we could not sleep. The bullock cart swayed from side to side, transferring all the shocks of the uneven road to our bodies. It was pitch dark outside, with only a tiny kerosene lantern lighting the front side of the cart, probably just bright enough for the driver to see the road ahead. I suppose the two bullocks that pulled the cart did so instinctively, without much goading from the driver. I kept anticipating the thrill of seeing a railway train for the first time in my life. After reaching Pattambi, we waited for the train to arrive, and eventually it did, after a couple of hours.

I can still recall the great excitement I felt when I saw the train steaming into the station. Since it was my very first train journey, I thoroughly enjoyed it. And after reaching Trichy, the sights and sounds of buses, cars, traffic signals and the hustle and bustle of city traffic overwhelmed me. A whole new urban world opened up before my eyes for the very first time in my life. It was, for me, a truly memorable experience.

The second event that brought me in contact with the world outside my village was a leg injury I suffered while running to school. A rock had hit me on the shin of my right leg and the resulting open wound bled profusely. I suppose my father then administered some preliminary first aid and bandage. The wound kept growing bigger and bigger for weeks, and simply would not heal. My father kept cleaning the wound regularly, putting boric powder and some other medication on it. The wound continued to cause a lot of pain and suffering. I limped for several weeks. There were no antibiotics or other modern medication available around the house or in our village.

One day, I went along with my father to Karinganad to see my grandparents, limping all the way. When I reached there, my Uncle Chinnanna asked me why I was limping so much. He started to open the bandage around the wound so that he could inspect it. And when he saw the wound, he said he could not believe his eyes. He became very emotional and started sobbing profusely and uncontrollably. It appeared that the wound had become very large indeed, had turned septic, and the whole area around the middle part of the leg was badly infected. He said he was going to take me to the hospital at once; otherwise, he argued, the infection would become dangerous.

Without any hesitation, he carried me on his shoulders and walked about ten miles to the nearest hospital in Trithala. I was too confused to argue with him. He deposited me in the doctor's office, and the next day they operated on my leg. It seemed that without immediate surgery, the wound would never heal, as the whole area surrounding it had become badly infected. A whole piece of flesh from the shin had to be cut away by the surgeon. The bone around the wound had to be scrapped. It took about four weeks for me to recover from the surgery, and the tissue around the bone left a huge scar, which became a major identifying mark on my person ever since.

In keeping with our religious beliefs and customs (which I explained earlier), Amma later took me to Guruvayur temple to worship Lord Krishna and offer prayers and thanks for healing my wound. The temple at Guruvayur (about twenty miles from Karinganad) is famous throughout Kerala. This act of piety further reinforced my religious beliefs, and I became a devotee of Lord Krishna.

# Chapter 4

## High School Years

In 1947, after completing the eighth grade education in Rayira-nellur School, my father enrolled me in National High School, Pattambi. This school was about eight miles from Vilayur. For a while, I walked to school on alternate days. The walk took about 2 to 2.5 hours in each direction. We could not afford to go by bus to school every day, even though the bus fare was nominal, about half a rupee per day. To minimize the walking distance, father decided to send me to Karinganad to stay with my grandparents. The distance from there to Pattambi was about six miles. For the next three years, I stayed there and continued my high school studies.

1947 was the year India gained independence from British rule. I was twelve years old then. The country was caught up in the frenzy of Independence Day celebrations. The leaders of the independence movement, Gandhi and Nehru, were household names throughout India. We were thrilled to participate in the national euphoria. There were speeches, dramas, cultural festivals and parades for several days. It all seemed like a dream, because I really could not appreciate nor understand the full significance of these events then, not having learned about the history of British rule in India. But I started learning soon enough, as soon as I opened my eyes to the world of learning.

I think I really enjoyed my three years of high school education. I made lots of new friends. We had excellent teachers. They inspired us to learn. I soaked up as many facts, information and knowledge as I could. Our English teacher was the headmaster of the school. He immersed us in various books by Charles Dickens, Wordsworth and Tolstoy. Dickens's *Pickwick Papers* was his favorite book. I learned a lot by reading various essays written by innumerable British and American writers, such as Oliver Goldsmith, Samuel Johnson, Charles Lamb, David Thoreau and Benjamin Franklin. More than any other subject, I enjoyed learning geography. We had a fantastic teacher (whom we used to call TLR) who made it a great joy to study the world atlas and learn about different countries and cultures of the world. We learned about the great cities and civilizations of China and Europe. We traced the Trans Siberian Railway and the Orient Express. The names of the great rivers of Africa, America, China and India were etched in my memory forever. In my civics class, the book *Our India* by Minoo Masani taught me the shocking statistics that the average life expectancy of an Indian in 1945 was twenty-eight years! (Since then it has more than doubled, and recently reached about sixty-five).

I was not very fond of science subjects. I did not like physics, chemistry and botany very much. These were all required subjects. History was not particularly interesting for me, although we learned a great deal about ancient India and the 200 or so years of British Raj in India. I was not good in Mathematics either, though I scored decent marks in the final examinations. All students had to participate in various athletics. I suppose I barely made it through those classes. I was a weakling, I think. Malnutrition during my early childhood had taken its toll.

Among all the subjects I studied, the one I liked least was my own mother tongue, Malayalam. Although the medium of instruction was in Malayalam, I somehow did poorly in it, and did not pay much attention to learn it better. To this day, I have been somewhat awkward in using my own native tongue in speaking and writing. However, the beauty of some of the poems I learned in Malayalam still haunts me, and I can recall the power of that language in describing both nature and life at its best. I did enjoy reading many poems written in my native language by Kerala's three eminent poets—Vallathol, Asan and Ulloor.

Somehow I got into the habit of reading a lot, much beyond what was required for schoolwork. Whenever I visited my parents in Vilayur, I took books from my father's old collection and started reading them. Fortunately, father had a decent collection of various books by many eminent British writers. My lifelong habit of reading has served me well personally, intellectually and professionally. Some of my classmates even used to joke that I was a "book-worm." "There goes that bookworm," they used to shout behind my back.

Probably those three years of high school were the most forma-tive years of my student life. The habits I inculcated then have stayed with me ever since. Reading books by Mahatma Gandhi, Nehru, Tolstoy, Dickens, Goldsmith and other celebrated authors instilled in me a great love for the English language and its litera-ture. Truth, sincerity, determination, perseverance, self-confidence, fortitude and optimism were some of the characteristics delineated in these works, which I learned to adopt, practice and live by. To a large extent, I have been successful in following these noble prin-ciples throughout my life, though I have had ample failures, too, along the way. As I write this life story, I may be able to elaborate on these later as the occasions arise.

All the high school students in my group were required to take an "optional" subject in addition to all the mandatory ones. As per the advice of my father, I chose shorthand. The idea behind this was very practical and straightforward. During those years, stu-dents with skills in shorthand and typing were able to secure jobs with considerable ease. (Such is probably the case with students who are computer-literate nowadays.) Upon graduation from high school, I could go to a city like Bombay and get immediate em-ployment. Therefore, I elected to take shorthand as my optional subject.

I must say that we had a first-rate teacher in this subject as well. He really drilled us into the subtleties of Pitman's shorthand, and I became addicted to writing almost everything in shorthand by the time I graduated from high school. As an added bonus, I well remember the many fine English prose passages in the short-hand textbook we used to practice with. The beauty and clarity of those fine essays impressed me greatly, and I became familiar with many English authors who turned their writings into such a beauti-ful form of art. This too got me hooked to reading more and more, in order to enjoy the sheer beauty of the language, and the pleasure of learning from the great masters of literature.

Now I must digress a little to recount my family life in Karinganad during my high school years. We had a joint family system. Three of my uncles, with their wives and children, lived together with my grandparents under one roof. My grandmother was a very loving, affectionate person. She had complete control over the household, and ruled her little kingdom with an iron hand. She made sure that I got up early in the morning, probably around 6:30 (I am guessing, because there was no clock in the house). She would cook a simple but delicious meal for me every morning, and pack some lunch in a box for school. While she did this, I would take my bath, finish my prayers, and get dressed for school. Before leaving for school, all the children had to sit for about half an hour and say their prayers, recite the multiplication tables, and go through the ritual of repeating aloud several Malayalam poems. These poems had inherent moral values and spiritual content, although we did not comprehend them fully. This routine was mandatory in the evening too, before dinner, every day.

My grandfather patiently taught me the various Sanskrit Vedic mantras and prayers. He was a highly spiritual person, with deep religious convictions. He had led a very hard life and brought up a large family. All his children adored him; indeed, I should say, revered him. My memory of my beloved grandfather is that of a very tenderhearted and extremely indulgent individual. He took pains to teach me so many things about our culture and ways of life. In his old age, he presided over family (and social) functions such as anniversaries, marriages, birthdays and various religious ceremonies with great dignity. I know of no one else who led a simpler life in his or her old age. He always urged me to excel in my studies, as well as in other spheres of life. Until his death in 1950, just before the age of eighty, he continued to oversee the affairs of the joint family, and was the cementing force that kept it intact, glued together, and functioning amicably. I record with great pleasure and sincerity some of the moral and spiritual aspects of living that he taught me with so much affection.

These were the years when my lifelong habit of walking really took hold. Whenever my father or Uncle Chinnanna could afford

32

to give me money for the bus fare, I took the bus from the Karinganad bus stand to Pattambi. (Probably this was the case roughly twice a week.) Our house was about a mile away from the main road bus stand. Sometimes I would take the bus in the morning and walk back from school in the evening with other school mates. At other times, I would walk in the morning and take the bus for the return trip. I guess it depended on whether we could catch the bus in time, or whether the bus was already full of passengers with hardly any more room to accommodate a thin-bodied, frail student like myself. Indeed, many a time the bus conductor would squeeze a few more students into the crowded bus, and leave some of us behind to walk. Sometimes the bus would be so full that the conductor could not walk through the bus to collect the student's fare! Consequently we would get a free ride by default.

From the Karinganad bus stand to Pattambi was a distance of about five miles, which we could walk in less than two hours. There were three or four students, besides myself, who walked together as a group. Unlike most eighth grade students in the United States, who seem to carry so many books and other paraphernalia in their backpacks when they go to school, we did not have much to carry in our tiny book bags. Nor could we afford to buy all the books even when they were necessary or required. So walking the distance to school was not a problem, except that on several occasions the inside of my unprotected feet got badly hurt by the ubiquitous bamboo thorns, glass pieces or other debris on the road. Then it would hurt and I would suffer for days, until the sores healed naturally.

My school campus consisted of a cluster of buildings with thatched roofs. Most of the buildings were long halls, with hardly any walls dividing the individual classrooms. During the monsoon season, torrential rains would drench the classrooms. Sometimes the roofs leaked a lot, with water leaking down on our benches. In fact those classrooms were only nominally divided from each other by thick bamboo mats, which were hung from the ceiling. Sometimes the noise and chatter from other classrooms could be heard in our classes. Big blackboards for the teachers were set up on improvised stands, and were not integrated with the walls of the classrooms (because there were no walls at all!). Students were expected to clean the blackboards before the teachers walked into the classroom. All the students would stand up respectfully as soon as the teachers walked in, and would take up their seats only after the teacher signaled them to sit. Boys and girls sat in separate parts of the room, with hardly any interaction between the two sexes. Classes usually ran from 9 a.m. to 4 p.m. with a small lunch break in between. Most classes had about forty students. By and large, they were an obedient bunch. I cannot remember many acts of disobedience on the part of students. In general, the school worked very smoothly.

At the end of the day, we would walk back home or take the bus if I had the bus fare in my pocket. We would reach home between 6 and 7 p.m. Soon after reaching home, grandmother would give me a snack and tea. However, I could not enter the house until I took a bath in the pond. Only then was I allowed to enter inside the house premises. School clothes were left in a designated room, to be worn again the next day. Entering the house wearing those clothes was not allowed. Going to school and mingling with outsiders was considered "ayithom," or bodily pollution, similar to the concept of untouchability. (Note: There is no easy way for me to interpret or translate this colloquial word. In each and every language, there are some idioms or expressions that defy translation into another language.)

With the benefit of hindsight, I can now appreciate that the strict enforcement of this custom kept the house relatively free from germs and external contaminants. This was especially the case in an environment where modern disinfectants or medical protection against contagious diseases was not available. We now know that many of the ancient customs and practices of our ancestors, which we used to misunderstand, abhor or make fun of, actually made a lot of sense in their time and place. It has taken me a lot of years and careful reflection to appreciate the truth! "Live and learn," as they say.

Like almost everyone else, one of the major difficulties that I faced during my high school years was a lack of money to do certain simple things or participate in some activities dear to the hearts of youngsters. A couple of instances stick out in my mind. There was not enough money to buy kerosene to keep the lamps lighted for reading beyond the customary bedtime of around nine o'clock. Even when I had to study for an examination the next day, I was expected to go to bed early because kerosene was in such shortage, and the price so high, that keeping the light on for studying an extra hour or so was out of the question.

Another minor detail worth recording is that there were two types of kerosene available at that time: white and red. The white kerosene was more expensive, but burned better, without leaving a trail of black soot. The red variety was cheaper, but would smell bad, and worse, left hard-to-clean black soot on the glass lamp enclosing the wicker. When money was especially tight, we had to settle for the red kerosene, which everyone abhorred, but the alternative was total darkness.

When many of my other classmates went on an excursion to Trichur to see the Pooram Festival (celebrated for its unique spectacle of several caparisoned elephants in procession, flanked by "panchavadyam"—a symphony consisting of different musical instruments and five distinct varieties of native drums—played by a band of percussionists and orchestra players), I was unable to go because I could not come upon a few rupees for the journey. I must have cried for hours because of this perceived deprivation! (This is one of my cherished wishes that yet remains to be fulfilled).

* * *

NOTE: The Pooram Festival is an extraordinarily beautiful spectacle. It has won worldwide recognition for its marvelous display of decorated elephants, pageantry and grandeur, unparalleled anywhere else in the world. It is, without a doubt, a must-see event, which has few equals elsewhere.

The other big event in Kerala that attracts a great deal of attention is the Onam Boat Race held in Alleppey. These great and beautiful rowboats are handmade with utmost care from lightweight bamboo, coconut fiber and other local woods. Rows upon rows of these beautiful, handcrafted boats take part in the annual boat race. It is televised throughout India. The competition is intense, and the event is celebrated with great pomp.

* * *

On one occasion, I was thrown out of school because I could not pay the monthly fee of six and a half rupees. I was, however, reinstated in school after my father came up with the money in a few days.

All in all, those three years of high school went very smoothly. I learned a great deal, and got an excellent grounding in those fundamental academic subjects, which constitute the foundation for one's preparation for life's journey. I finished high school in March 1950, when I was about fifteen years old.

Now that my high school education was completed, the question arose as to what the next step should be. I spent a few months idling away in Vilayur. There I was, helping father with farming, tending the cattle, doing many household chores and pondering over what to do with my life. In school, I had no doubt learned shorthand exceedingly well, but not typing. Without a working knowledge of typing, one could not become a stenographer, which was the occupation father had in mind for me. And there was no typewriting institute nearby to learn this important professional skill. So, after some deliberation, and in consultation—through correspondence—with my Uncle Ponnanna, who was in Bangalore working as an accountant in the Indian Defense Department, I was sent there to learn typing and possibly to find a job.

It was in Bangalore that I learned bicycling for the first time. I slowly began to cope with the stress and strain of living in an urban setting. In a few months, I also learned how to type, but not proficiently enough to secure any remunerative employment. I did not get any job. I guess my extremely youthful appearance (I was hardly sixteen years old then), as well as my untested job skills, may have scared away potential employers. Dejected and dispirited, I returned home to Vilayur, because my Uncle Ponnanna

36

could not afford to keep me much longer under his care.

Once again I was in my home turf, but without any moorings. After consulting with my Aunt Parukutty in the city of Cochin (about seventy miles away), father sent me there to improve my typing skills. For five months I stayed with her. She was extremely generous and loving, and did her best to encourage me to become proficient in typing. After completing the first typing examination, but without securing a job, I returned to Vilayur, empty-handed!

For the next year or so, I led an idyllic life in the village. My elder brother, Mani, was at this time a schoolteacher in Vilayur. Father and Mani were both earning members of the family. They decided to send me to the typewriting institute in Perintalmanna, about ten miles away from home, to prepare for the Higher Level Examination in typing. Without such a credential, it may have been difficult to secure a good job. So I journeyed from Vilayur to Perintalmanna two or three times a week, walking one way and taking the bus for the return trip. During this time, I helped my father (indirectly) by representing him at the local Sub-Treasury Office in Perintalmanna to cash his monthly school salary vouchers. Since he was the manager of the Vilayur School, he was responsible for collecting and disbursing the monthly salaries of the teachers. I felt very responsible and important carrying all that cash in my bag.

To hone my stenography skills, father and Mani would dictate to me long passages from books and newspapers, which I would write down in shorthand. I would then read back what I had scribbled. I also secured some advanced books in shorthand, which helped me considerably in improving my transcribing skills.

It was now time for me to take the examinations necessary to get certification in stenography. I was sent to Calicut, which was the headquarters of the Malabar District examination center. I appeared for the examinations, and passed them with flying colors. Now, at last, I was certified to be employable as a stenographer. The only problem was to secure a job.

In order to get a decent, well-paying job, I had to leave Kerala. I was almost seventeen years old by then. Where would I go? How would I secure a job initially?

Fortunately, my Uncle Kunchanna promised to help finance my trip in search of employment. The elders held a conference and decided to send me to Secunderabad, where my Uncle Ponnanna was then working. They thought it would be best for me to have the guidance of an experienced person like Ponnanna. So, in November 1952, I proceeded to Secunderabad, and joined my uncle's household once again.

Pounding the streets of Secunderabad every day, I soon found a job with a film distribution firm. I worked there for about four months. The job paid only eighty rupees per month, which was insufficient for my own living expenses in the city. Therefore, I continued my quest for a better-paying job, which I landed soon enough. With my uncle's permission and blessings, I took leave of his family and moved to Hyderabad to join my new employer. (By the way, Secunderabad and Hyderabad are known as the "twin cities." Just like Minneapolis and St. Paul, they are adjacent to each other).

For the next four years, I worked as a stenographer with Hind Tobacco Company. The starting salary was 110 rupees, which was a great improvement over my first job. I moved into a hotel, called Neo Mysore Café, which housed several young workingmen like me. I had two other roommates, and one of them taught me Yoga. Ever since I have practiced yoga, almost all my life.

Our lifestyle in Hyderabad was enjoyable and interesting. We played a lot of badminton, took walks around the beautiful Public Gardens in Hyderabad, and saw lots of Hindi movies. It was in Hyderabad that I learned to speak Hindi, India's national language.

Oh, I almost forgot to say that for the first time in my life I started wearing shoes at the age of seventeen. This was required as part of the office attire. At first, my feet ached a lot. I think some blisters developed on my feet thanks to those new shoes. My feet had to get accustomed to wearing them. For a while the new footwear felt really awkward. Perhaps my feet felt like they were being put in some kind of feet prison! I couldn't wait to get out of those shoes as soon as I returned home from work.

Eventually, after some struggle, I got used to wearing them. They were no longer a novelty to my feet. It is funny how our life-long habits can change beyond belief. Nowadays I am unable to walk without shoes anywhere outside the house. Indeed, I cannot live without them. One gets used to almost everything: walking without shoes for almost seventeen years, and then not being able to walk without them at all for the rest of your life!

# Chapter 5

## Some Post-Secondary Education

After settling down into my new job, I began to think seriously about higher studies. The desire to study and get ahead in life had somehow become an obsession with me. I knew that a regular college education was out of my reach, because of the necessity to work full time during the day. At that time, there were no evening college classes available for working people like me. What was I to do? Fortunately, I learned about an opportunity to write the intermediate examination (similar to an associate's degree after two years of college courses) in Ajmer, conducted by the Board of Higher Education in Rajasthan. I could prepare for the examination through a self-study program. Eagerly, I sought information about the required syllabus, courses of study and textbooks. I chose commerce as my main subject, because by now I had realized that for a person like me, without a first-rate knowledge of mathematics or science subjects, commerce/economics would be the most practical entrance to better employment opportunities as well as income. I decided to devote all my spare time to study and prepare for the examination. For the next two years, I self-taught all the required subjects: English, history, accounting, commerce and economics. At last, I thought I was ready to take the examinations, and informed the board that I would go to Bhopal, the nearest examination center, to take them. This was in 1954, and I was almost twenty years old.

The examinations were to be held in the Government Hamidia College, Bhopal. (This is a city about 500 miles north of Hyderabad). The examinations were scheduled over a period of five days. I journeyed to Bhopal, stayed in a local hostel, and appeared for the examinations. I unburdened myself of all the tension and strain I had accumulated over the past two years. Not knowing what to expect in the examinations, and not having anyone to guide me, I thought I did the best I could under the circumstances. When the

41

five-day ordeal was finished, I wanted nothing better than to get away from it all. There was very little left for me to do but wait for the results to be announced in about two months.

Earlier, I had heard of Sanchi and the great Buddhist Stupa near Bhopal. I told myself that I deserved a good holiday, and I took the opportunity to take the next available train to Hoshangabad, near Sanchi, to visit the Stupa. I started from Bhopal early in the morning so that I could see Sanchi and return before nightfall, then take the train back to Hyderabad the following morning. I really enjoyed seeing the formidable Stupa, one of the greatest examples of ancient Indian architecture, and was awestruck by its beauty, design and surroundings. I got so carried away by it all that when I reached Hoshangabad railway station for the return trip to Bhopal around 6 p.m., the train had just left the station.

Probably for the first time in my life, I felt somewhat confused and did not know what to do next. I had no plans to stay overnight in Hoshangabad, and probably could not have done so anyway because I had neither the money nor the leave from my office to do so. What was I to do? My mind started racing. The next train was not until 10.30 p.m. I had about four hours to wait. If I walked to Bhopal along the railway line, it would take me just about three hours to cover the ten-mile distance. I decided to walk, and I had probably never, ever walked as fast as I did on that night. It became dark very soon. I was alone. There was nobody to tell me not to do this. Suddenly, I felt a calmness of mind and courage such as I had never felt before. Or so I imagined, just to boost my spirits. I had no idea about the ordeal ahead of me. I was extremely hungry and tired. I had wandered through Sanchi all day, enjoying the marvelous scenes and the architectural wonders of the Stupa (so I was already exhausted from all that walking). I guess after walking along the rail tracks for an hour or so, I must have felt foolish about my decision to walk rather than wait for the next train. But it was too late for such ruminations. I couldn't turn back. There was only one thing to do, and that was to continue my walk to the bitter end; my destination, Bhopal.

This experience taught me several things about myself. I had made a hasty decision to walk, without anticipating the difficulties that lay ahead. I thought I had more reserves of energy and strength than I really had. It did not occur to me to carry food or water for such a long ordeal. (Of course there was no bottled water in those days to carry around). I should have eaten something in the railway station before starting my arduous journey, but it did not occur to me at all. I was so wrapped up in thinking about getting back to Bhopal as soon as possible that I forgot that the entire distance would be devoid of any store to buy food or drinks. The railroad tracks ran through absolutely barren land and uninhabited areas. As the evening wore on and sunlight slowly began to diminish, I grew apprehensive about the task ahead of me. This was a completely different experience from anything I had known earlier. Because I was walking through open countryside, dimly lit by the night stars, I could see the long railway line ahead of me. It stretched like an endless long ribbon of steel. The outline of the land on either side of the tracks was barely visible except for some trees. I was getting somewhat afraid of my surroundings, to say the least. I tried to focus my mind on reaching Bhopal as quickly as possible. Tired, thirsty, hungry, anxious and fearful, I kept moving forward to my destination. By the time I reached there, I was so exhausted and weary that I could hardly finish the meal I had ordered, even though I remember eating like a pig, as they say. Immediately afterward, I went to bed, and slept like a log, or as a little baby would after being fully fed by its mother.

I woke up the next morning, boarded the train and returned to Hyderabad to resume my job.

I had paid dearly for my thoughtlessness. I could blame nobody but myself for the predicament I put myself in. Perhaps, as a result of this experience, I learned to think clearly about the consequences of one's decisions before embarking on a course of action. It was a lesson well learned, I think. I will have a lot more to say later about the importance of proper decision making in life.

I remember this foolish episode as one of the highlights of my life's experiences. I recount it whenever someone asks me about a memorable adventure in my life.

# Chapter 6

## Life in Hyderabad

During the next four years 1952 to 1956, I matured mentally as a young man, capable of taking care of myself. I learned a lot about life, its trials and tribulations. Probably my personal growth as an individual and my subsequent philosophical outlook on different aspects of life were developed around this time. The lifestyle that evolved during that period gradually became embedded in my personality forever.

Self-help became my new religious creed. Probably the most important book that has influenced my life is *Self Help* by Samuel Smiles. I adopted the author's prescription to depend on oneself throughout life, and take responsibility for both one's successes and failures in everything we do. This philosophy seemed to me to make a lot of sense. Blaming others, including God, and selectively ascribing our failures to "fate" or "bad luck" seemed to be an easy excuse at best. I gradually eschewed the popular Hindu point of view that our "karma"—the accumulated result of our past actions in our earlier lives (both good and bad), controlled our destiny in our present life. This did not satisfy me at all. I did not like the idea of "this present life" of ours owing anything to a supposed "previous life." It seemed only rational that we should do our very best in all our personal endeavors here and now. I decided to depend on others as little as possible. This point of view was further buttressed by reading several other biographies of leaders such as Napoleon, Churchill, Franklin, Lincoln, Gandhi and Nehru. I learned that every one of them charted out their individual courses of action, and chose to ignore difficulties that came along the way. Single-minded pursuit of one's goals, carefully chosen, and the determination to carry them out, was the guiding principle of their lives.

Two other essays of great significance that influenced me were

Emerson's piece on "Self Reliance" and Thoreau's *Walden*. I realized that every one of us has unlimited potential to determine the course of our lives and to achieve our goals if we pursue them wholeheartedly. The dictum of "maximum self help" suited my circumstances very well. I realized that it was up to me, and no one else, to do what I had to do to get ahead.

This newfound philosophy of self-reliance was, in some ways, completely alien to me until now. It was a revelation. I now adopted it with great enthusiasm. During the previous ten years of my life, I had been taught that the particular circumstances of our life depended on God's will, or the result of our own past karma. Therefore, most of my actions were guided by fear and subservience to higher authority—be it God, parents, elders, teachers or employers. By and large, I was under the influence of various superstitious beliefs that were inculcated in me from early childhood. I was under the impression that success or failure in everything I did was dependent on whether or not my personal Goddess was pleased or displeased by my actions.

At last I found myself almost free from this karmic bondage. It was a remarkable transformation in my thinking. Not only was I free from any supervision by my parents or elders, but also from many other superstitious beliefs. This newfound wisdom, this new personal freedom, this wonderful philosophy was exhilarating. It allowed me to do what I chose to do, for my personal growth, well being and mental development. From now on, I was responsible for everything I did in life, whether good or bad. No one else but myself had responsibility for the outcome. "The buck stops here," indeed, as President Truman said. I was now determined to shape my future.

Before I explain what I did with this new line of thinking, let me take a small detour here.

* * *

A little bit of history about Hyderabad is in order at this point. During the time of British rule, there were more than 400 princely states in India. Some of them were very large in size, and among the largest was Hyderabad, ruled by the autocratic Nina. The British government had conferred upon him the title of "HEH"—His Exalted Highness—the Nizam of Hyderabad and Berar, a title he adorned with much pride. No other Indian king or prince had such a grand-sounding title. Before Indian independence, Hyderabad was one of those few princely states that had its own currency, called the Hali Scicca. When I arrived there in 1952, this local currency was still in circulation, side by side with the Indian rupee. Employees could be paid either in HS or rupees, whichever they preferred. The HS continued to be used for a few more years, and was demonetized gradually.

Hyderabad had become a part of the Indian Union only after a brief diplomatic struggle with the proud and autocratic ruler, Nizam. He was determined to retain his status as an absolute, independent monarch. However, the Indian Central Government in New Delhi could not agree to this, and launched the euphemistically called "police action," annexing the state to the Indian Union without ceremony. During the time I was a resident there, the Nizam's erstwhile power and prestige were still very much in evidence. Many of the rules and regulations of the old kingdom were still in vogue.

Among the Nizam's proud showpieces is the Salar Jung Museum in Hyderabad, with a world-class collection of several works of art, sculptures and other potpourri of precious artifacts collected painstakingly from around the world during his regime. The museum's collections are rare, magnificent, and many of them are one-of-a-kind. This outstanding world-heritage museum is well worth a visit.

* * *

I now return to my life in Hyderabad. Walking as much as possible (for exercise and physical well being) became one of the habits I adopted as a guiding principle. My office was about a mile and a half away from my lodge, and the usual mode of transportation I chose was walking. I familiarized myself with the geography of Hyderabad very well. I used to walk a lot along the King Kothi

Road, a winding, beautiful path surrounding the Nizam's Palace. One of the well-known and much photographed landmarks of Hyderabad is the Char Minar, at the periphery of Sultan Bazar, where my office was located. The words stand for "four minarets," an impressive structure (built about 400 years ago) that served as the entrance gate to the Old City. The Hussain Sagar Lake is a large and beautiful body of water, along which was built the Tank Bund Road, connecting the twin cities of Secunderabad and Hyderabad. Often I used to walk along this road enjoying the wonderful evening breeze while watching the sunset on the distant horizon. Several rich and famous people of the city lived on the far side of this lake. My boss lived in one of the mansions in the adjoining wealthy neighborhood called Somajiguda. I used to frequent his palatial house whenever he called me there for some office-related work. The famous Golconda fort, the dilapidated old capital city of the erstwhile Bhamini dynasty (which ruled the Deccan during the time of the Mughal emperor Aurangazeb in the 1700s), situated about thirty miles from Hyderabad, was also a spot I visited frequently.

My boss (whom we respectfully referred to as BP), a very wealthy industrialist of Hyderabad, was a patron of the arts. He was deeply interested in various kinds of ancient and modern art, of which I was ignorant at that time. He was a friend of MF Hussain and Jagdish Mittal, two of the most eminent artists of modern India. Very frequently he used to purchase different works of art by these painters as well as others. Although I was unaware of the significance of these transactions at the time, I picked up some rudimentary knowledge about art and painting through my association with BP. He used to subscribe to many arts magazines, as well as numerous other publications such as the *National Geographic* and the *Manchester Guardian*. Glancing through some of these magazines during my spare time, I became more aware of the world at large. My dormant interest in geography, my favorite subject during high school years, was rekindled by reading articles in the *National Geographic*. On one occasion, I glanced at an article about New Zealand, and as a result, I developed a deep interest in visiting that country to see its beautiful landscape and study its

Maori culture. To travel around the world and see for myself different countries and cultures became one of my cherished ambitions. (I am glad to say that this desire has been partially satisfied after waiting for about forty years).

During this period, I watched many Hindi and English films. Watching movies regularly seemed to be my main source of entertainment. Two of the Hollywood movies I remember watching were, first, *California Conquest*, a Western, which spiked my interest in the American West; and second, *Samson and Delilah*, celebrated for its panoramic depiction of a biblical story. After watching these movies, I got hooked to Hollywood films, and must have seen lots of them in the next two or three years, as well as during the subsequent seven years when I lived in New Delhi. The Hindi film that captivated my interest the most was *Baiju Bawra*, and I was haunted by its scintillating music. I must have watched that movie about half a dozen times, without losing any of my initial interest. Another Hindi movie I watched several times was the musical *Anarkali*. There were scores of movie theatres in the city, and it became so easy and convenient to slip into one of them after supper, especially on a hot summer day. I picked up conversational Hindi pretty fast as a result of these frequent movie visits. I also enrolled in formal Hindi classes to learn the language, and completed two examinations within the next year. This helped me to familiarize myself with some Hindi literature, although I never gained proficiency in the language.

One of the regrets I have had in life is that I was not able to keep in touch with the few good friends of my early youth. They were the source of so many shared experiences, lengthy discussions and good times. Two of my high school friends completely disappeared from my life after I moved away from Vilayur. In Hyderabad, I had the good fortune to develop new friendships, and I derived a lot of satisfaction from closely associating with them. Without the familiar daily interaction with family members, which had been the hallmark of my life until then, I felt rather lonely, somewhat lost and ill at ease in my new environment. This vacuum was gradually filled by the abiding and deep friendships that de-

49

veloped anew. Although my Uncle Ponnanna in Secunderabad was a great source of comfort and closeness as a family member, I saw him only occasionally, whenever I could visit their home. Therefore, I was determined to cultivate my new friendships. I stayed in touch with them for several years after I moved to New Delhi in 1956.

* * *

I now return to the academic side of my life. I had obtained my Intermediate Certificate in Commerce early in 1955. This is akin to an associate's degree from a two-year college in the United States. I was again starting to feel frustrated, as there was no possibility of pursuing my academic interests side-by-side with working on a full-time job. Fortunately for me, just around that time Osmania University in Hyderabad decided to start an experimental evening college program for working people on the campus of Nizam's College, which was in the vicinity of my lodge. I eagerly enrolled in the program and started attending classes regularly at night. I chose commerce as my elective. The first year of study was about to be completed when I decided to move to New Delhi in search of a better job and higher pay.

Between the time I completed the Bhopal examination and my enrollment in the Osmania University program, I had appeared at the UPSC (Union Public Service Commission) examination for stenographers. This was needed to secure a government job. At that time, securing a central government job was thought to be desirable for reasons of job security, prestige and pay. The UPSC examination was conducted in Bombay during August 1955. It took almost seven months after the completion of this examination to announce the results. Early in March 1956 I was notified that I was selected, and was simultaneously offered employment in New Delhi at a much higher salary, about 250 rupees. This offer was far superior to my existing job, even though my current salary had inched up to almost 160 rupees (from the initial 120 rupees) during those four years.

However, making the move to New Delhi was not an easy de-

50

cision. There were two powerful factors that argued against the relocation.

My younger brother, Ramakrishnan, had just joined me in Hyderabad, and I was responsible to help him secure suitable employment there. Just like me, he had come to Hyderabad after completing his high school education and learning stenography in Kerala. The transition to urban life was not going to be easy for him either. My presence in Hyderabad was needed to familiarize him with his new environment, get him accustomed to city life, and to give him emotional support. At the time he arrived, I had no idea that I would soon be offered the opportunity to go to New Delhi. Fortunately, Ramakrishnan secured a job almost immediately upon his arrival. Therefore, I was partly free to consider seriously whether I would want to accept the New Delhi job offer. After much discussion between us, it was agreed that if I departed, my brother could follow me after a few months.

The other factor that weighed in favor of "staying put" in Hyderabad was the desire to continue my education. I had just completed one year in the BA Commerce program of Osmania University. It was not advisable to disrupt my studies, especially because if I moved to New Delhi all the credits (courses) I had completed would be nontransferable. In those days, transferring college credits from one institution to another in India was not easy, or even possible. I was in a quandary.

When confronted with difficult choices, one has to carefully consider the pros and cons of each available alternative. This is the kind of situation almost everyone encounters often in life. After much deliberation, I decided to make the move to New Delhi, leaving my brother to look after himself, and abandoning my commerce degree program unfinished. The main reason for this decision was economic. The attraction of secure government employment and the considerable increase in salary offered to me were the overriding attractions. I made a difficult choice, the precursor of many more such situations likely to come later in life. This is the stuff of which our lives are made. We have to be prepared for them all the time, for they are probably the only constants in life. The decisions we make drive the course of our lives. Winning or losing, success or failure, happiness or misery, profit or loss—all these things depend on how we choose.

In March 1956, I was about twenty-one years old and had lived in Secunderabad/Hyderabad for almost four years. I was by then attuned to urban life, and could speak Hindi, the language of Northern India, quite fluently. I had a good grounding in office work. I was eager to try and experience new challenges. I was confident of my own abilities. With the help of an introductory letter from my friend Anantharaman, I would be able to spend a few days as a guest with a member of his family in New Delhi. With these assets in hand, I boarded the train to New Delhi, leaving behind my brother, lots of fond memories and good friends. Although I was anxious about the outcome of my choice to move north, I was also very hopeful about my future.

* * *

AN IMPORTANT FOOTNOTE:

About forty-five years after leaving Hyderabad, I revisited my favorite city in 2001. I was eager to find out how the place had changed and also relive my old memories. I had to search very hard to locate the places I thought I knew so well. There was no longer the New Mysore Cafe Lodge where I used to live. The land on which the lodge stood had been transformed into a new multi-storied apartment complex. No one, except me, knew that a hostel had existed there once upon a time for many years. Nor could I locate my old office building on Sultan Bazaar. New construction had totally changed the appearance of that area. It was now difficult to walk the distance from my old lodge near Abid's Corner to my old office building in Sultan Bazaar because of traffic jams and congestion. The picture I had etched in my mind about the old Hyderabad was no longer a reality. The city I knew so well had grown beyond recognition. The three landmarks that I had known earlier, i.e., the Char Minar, the Hussain Sagar Lake and the dilapidated Golconda Fort, were the only things that had not changed. They have been there for centuries past, and probably will continue to exist as landmarks.

This trip back through memory lane was revealing. Our notions and ideas about people and places can often be misleading. Almost everything changes over time. Our memories play tricks on us. I had similar experiences when I visited my native Kerala village in 2006. What I thought was very familiar to me seemed very strange and distant. I was a total stranger in my own house—where I had spent many years of my childhood. Only my youngest brother and his family still live there. I guess I too had changed beyond recognition. Not only was my physical appearance very different now, but more importantly a completely different mind was now encased in my old body. This is probably what happens to all of us as we live our lives and grow old.

\* \* \*

After spending two nights on the train from Hyderabad, I reached New Delhi. After much fumbling and searching for the house of my host family in Karol Bagh (a suburb of New Delhi), I located their place. Their warm reception and hospitality pleased me greatly. After staying with them for a couple of days, and making a few inquiries about available lodging in the vicinity, I checked into nearby Mahadevan's Lodge as a paying guest. I stayed there for almost a year, until my move to more permanent quarters elsewhere.

The next chapter describes my adjustment to a different, new environment in New Delhi, and how I met the many challenges that lay in store for me.

# Chapter 7

## Government Employment in New Delhi

An old chapter of my life had just ended, and a new one had begun. The appointment I was offered in New Delhi was as a stenographer in the offices of All India Radio (AIR), which was a branch of the Ministry of Information and Broadcasting. The office was located in Broadcasting House, an architecturally beautiful building on Parliament Street, very close to the Indian Parliament House.

I was assigned to work with an Engineer-cum-Bureaucrat, Mr. Balu. He had just returned from the U.S. after an extended training course and had brought with him several books and informational material about America. They were scattered about in his office. I eagerly scanned the contents of those books and became quite knowledgeable about the geography, history and living conditions in America for the first time. Soon afterward, the idea germinated in my mind that I, too, should visit the U.S.A. sometime in my life. Little did I know then that most of my future life would be spent there!

The office work in AIR was quite different from what I was used to doing in Hyderabad earlier, although both jobs required stenography. My old boss, BP, gave me plenty of opportunities to develop my varied intellectual interests and become acquainted with worldly affairs. I found the atmosphere around my new job and the office environment much more constraining. I had to sit in the office, with very little freedom to move around, even when there was little work to do. But soon enough, I discovered a nearby resource to satisfy my curiosity about reading and learning. There was a library in Broadcasting House, and I helped myself liberally to its contents by checking out various books. I devoured many books by Churchill, PG Wodehouse and numerous other novels. I became addicted to the Wodehouse character Jeeves, and his

55

unique style of coping with the problems of life and interpersonal relationships. I must have read a dozen books by Wodehouse, and pictured in my mind the old British aristocratic lifestyle that the author delineated so well in the character of Bertie Wooster. Another book that impressed me a great deal was Churchill's *A History of English Speaking Peoples*. It was a pleasure to read, and I acquired a great deal of knowledge about how Britain established its worldwide empire on which "the Sun never sets."

My old habit of discovering the geography of my surroundings through long walks continued. Names of the numerous tree-lined, broad avenues of New Delhi—named after the various Mughal rulers and British viceroys—became gradually familiar to me within a few months. I frequented almost all the well-known landmarks of Delhi such as the Qutub Minar, Chandni Chowk, Red Fort, Jantar Mantar and Lodhi Gardens, as well as the innumerable historical forts and mosques scattered through the surrounding areas. Connaught Place, with its elegant, circularly columned buildings and wide expanse of small parks in between them, became a frequent haunt of mine. I drank a lot of tea in the many restaurants near the sidewalks, in the company of an office colleague, who became a very good friend. This was a happy, jolly, carefree period in my life.

My brother Ramakrishnan duly arrived in New Delhi a few months after I settled there. By this time, some of the residents in Mahadeven's Lodge, including myself, had become disenchanted with the hotel food and the quality of the fare they offered. A few of my friends and I got together and decided to move into a rented apartment, hiring a cook of our own and starting a joint "mess." (This term, mess, meant a common boarding arrangement for bachelors like us, or for people living together in a dorm. It is interesting that words can have such a different meaning in different contexts and places. Indeed, the term mess was used by Indian Army officers to describe their eating places in the barracks).

We all wanted such a change, and decided to make the move, which we did sometime in 1957. From then on, until I left New Delhi in 1963, we continued to live with our mess arrangement

56

quite successfully. I was in charge of running the mess and took care of its financial management. We hired an excellent cook and caretaker by the name of Sridharan. Not only was he a good cook, but also a savvy shopper and housekeeper. All of us enjoyed his cooking, and we had lots of fun living together for almost six years. Occasionally we held parties late into the night, with lots of hard liquor and beer, which we drank until some of us got into a stupor. Fortunately, these parties were infrequent, and everyone stayed indoors after drinking. We had a grand time without causing any trouble to anybody outside.

I found the daily routine of office work thoroughly boring. There was absolutely no challenge in my work. The office atmosphere was stifling, to say the least. I began to realize that unless I changed my occupation and got into something more interesting, the current job would lead to a dead end. Therefore, when the opportunity arose, I appeared for another UPSC examination. Successful candidates in the examination would be eligible to be drawn into a pool of "Secretariat Officers' Cadre" with good prospects for career advancement. I took the examination and awaited my chances.

Around this time, I was becoming obsessed with my balding head. Even before I left Hyderabad, the front of my hairline was receding rapidly, causing me great anxiety. By age twenty, I was becoming quite visibly bald. Probably my anxiety and worry caused the baldness to advance even more rapidly. I was thoroughly dismayed by my appearance. Nobody I knew had baldness at such a young age. I used to apply different oils and hair treatments to arrest the condition, and it only became worse day by day. The hair on my head simply did not want to stay there, no matter what I did to stop the "de-forestation." I did not know what to do. In desperation, on the advice of some hair expert, I started shaving my head (like the then-famous Hollywood actor Yul Brynner), and used to walk around in public with a hat on my pate.

I was under the impression that this desperate remedy of head shaving would surely make the hair grow back on my head. The baldness had made me very self-conscious and somewhat ashamed of my physical appearance. I used to think that no woman would ever want to marry me because of my bald head. It is no exaggeration to say that no other problem had engaged my attention as much as my baldness. By age twenty-five, I had become so visibly bald that I thought I looked ugly because of it. All my friends used to tell me that it did not matter in the least, but I refused to believe them. What was to be done? I was thoroughly disillusioned, unhappy and angry with myself. I could not easily accept my present appearance. At that time, my greatest envy was reserved for men with thick, black hair. I continued to think that a head full of hair was the choicest gift of God. Other men of my age took that for granted! I now realize, belatedly, that all the mental energy and time I had spent worrying about my hair was utterly useless and unproductive. Unfortunately, all of us habitually spend a great deal of our precious time and resources on the vast wasteland of utterly foolish pursuits. Our real or imagined frustrations with what we lack occupy our minds. This is the human condition—and it is undeniably one of the greatest tragedies of life.

Gradually I began to wonder about my future again. The realization dawned on me that if I did not continue my studies earnestly, I would not be able to make much headway in my professional life. No doubt I had a reasonably good salary, a secure job, and good prospects for modest career advancement. However, some inner drive, which I could not account for, urged me to continue my studies. Also, a university degree would be an important asset to have in advancing my career in federal government service. Many of the senior positions would have been available only to employees with a college degree. So, after making appropriate inquiries, I decided to enroll in the Punjab University Camp College in their Economics Honors program. This would enable me to graduate in two years. Punjab University did not recognize, nor give credit, for the courses I had taken in Hyderabad.

Soon my hitherto laid-back lifestyle began to change. It became very hectic and structured. After attending office from ten to five, I would trek from Parliament Street to Birla Mandir Marg where the evening college was located. This was a distance of about two miles, and I got my evening exercise by walking. Classes were held from about 6 to 9 p.m., three days a week. There was a lot of reading to do. My time passed very fast. Except during weekends or holidays, I had no time to wander around the city or do other extra-curricular activities. My acquaintances started making fun of me, and often chided me for my Spartan lifestyle. But I knew that I had a mission to accomplish, and I did not pay much attention to their jokes. After completing two years of study, I finished the BA Honors in Economics in 1959.

Soon after I completed the BA degree, another good opportunity presented itself for continuing my education. For the first time, Delhi University started in 1959 a postgraduate evening college program for working people. This was a "God-sent" chance for me. I had to decide which subject I should pick as my elective. Although I felt equally interested in English literature, political science and economics, I chose economics because I thought it seemed to offer greater challenge and opportunities for career advancement. I had no inkling at that time that I would one day become a professional economist. Thus began the two-year degree program at Delhi University, preparing me for the master's degree in Economics.

Whenever I could, I used to go around the university campus and observe daytime students and their activities in the various colleges. One of the academic activities I observed was debating. Debating between the various college teams fascinated me. I thought I too should try my skills in debating. We formed a debating society to represent our postgraduate evening college and I, along with a couple of other classmates, began to participate in these inter-collegiate debates. Soon this became a passion for me. I used to take leave from office work and attend various debating events. Our team won a couple of these debates, much to the delight of our college principal. I am proud to record that I represented my college in a debate with Punjab University in Panipat, and won a bundle of poetry books as a prize. I enjoyed reading that great collection of poems by Keats, Coleridge and Milton for many years.

Another interesting thing I did was to enter an essay competition for college students sponsored by the Congress for Cultural Freedom. The title of the essay competition was "Significance of the Life and Work of Tolstoy." Tolstoy was one of the authors we had studied in high school. I had enjoyed reading abbreviated versions of some of his books, as well as a couple of his novels while I was in Hyderabad. Therefore, I was intrigued by the prospect of entering the essay competition. It turned out to be a golden opportunity for me. I read as many of Tolstoy's books and literary criticism of his works as I could lay my hands on. I learned a great deal from this great master of story telling about Russian life.

I wrote the essay. I tried to refine it, improve it, and embellish it as much as possible. I submitted my essay. I was delightfully surprised when it was announced that I won the prize, and was awarded Rs.500 in a public ceremony held at Sapru House and presided over by Prime Minister Nehru. This was indeed one of the highlights of my academic life.

I should say that by this time, my academic interests had certainly become of paramount importance in my life. I became less and less interested in the office job, and concentrated most of my energies in studying for the MA final examinations. Office work became simply a means of earning a livelihood, and little else.

The daily grind became quite intense. The university campus was about twelve miles away from my office on Parliament Street. I used to board a bus around 5.30 p.m. that would take me to my destination in about forty-five minutes. Classes were held three times a week. After class, around 9 p.m., I would board a bus to our place in Karol Bagh, reaching home by about 10 p.m. Since all my friends would have finished their dinners early, I ate alone, which was not much fun. Then I devoted an hour or two for studying. There was a lot to study. Many weekends were spent in the Delhi School of Economics library in the university campus. Days passed swiftly, and before I knew it, examination time approached in March 1961.

There were eight subjects in the Economics curriculum. I really enjoyed my study hours at the Delhi School of Economics library.

I didn't mind my daily grind during those two years. There was not much time for activities other than the dull work at the office, coupled with my newfound academic interests. I got used to the tight schedule. It made me more disciplined, focused and results-oriented. I prepared extremely well for the ensuing final examinations, and was confident of my securing a first class. (Note: A "first class" connotes superior academic performance in Indian university parlance—akin to a "Straight A" grade in America).

I finished the examinations and awaited the results, which were to be announced in about two months. The next few months turned out to be some of the most eventful and challenging in my life.

By now, I had almost convinced myself that I should pursue my interest in economics in greater depth. I was beginning to be more and more interested in the subject. The courses I had taken in the MA program and the books I had read got me deeply interested in the subject. I had begun to regularly visit the Sapru House Library at the Indian School of International Studies. I also became a frequent visitor at the USIS (United States Information Service) and the British Council libraries, and started checking out many books on economics. At the same time, I slowly started looking into the possibility of applying for a scholarship for study abroad. Hoping to pursue my interest in economics, I solicited application forms and additional information from several foreign sources, one of which was the Commonwealth Scholarship Program to study in England. This scholarship required a first class master's degree. I had just completed my MA examinations, and nobody could predict whether or not I would secure a first class. But the application form indicated that as long as the applicant had a reasonable prospect of securing a first class, applications from potential candidates would be accepted, provisionally.

Now I faced a serious dilemma. If I did not apply for the scholarship right away (pending the results of the MA examination), the deadline for submitting the application could not be met. The results of the MA exam were not yet available. There was no time to wait. What should I do? Government employees were required to submit all applications for external jobs or scholarships through "proper channels," meaning with the explicit prior permission of the current employer. I was naïve, and thought that I could persuade my employer to forward my application, pending the announcement of the results of the MA exam.

I approached my boss and requested him to forward my application. The government bureaucracy began to churn its relentless process through "proper channels." My application was forwarded to the top administrator of AIR through the ranks. The top administrator refused to recommend me on the ground that there was no "reasonable proof" that I would secure a first class. I sought an interview with him, and argued that if indeed I could not secure a first class, the scholarship would be automatically denied to me; but that, nevertheless, I had a good chance of securing eligibility because I thought I had done extremely well in the examination. Since the MA examination results would not be available until the following week, the application had to be sent right away in order to meet the deadline. The top administrator would not relent. I could not persuade him to forward my application. I felt helpless, frustrated, and crestfallen. Perhaps for the second or third time in my life, I realized how it felt to be rejected—feeling like a failure. This sense of failure had first gripped my psyche when I was hunting for a job without success in Bangalore after completing my high school education.

There are many situations in life when people do strange, inexplicable, unfathomable things, the rationale for which we find difficult to understand. We wonder why someone would engage in these actions, which baffle the rest of us. Perhaps there are valid and persuasive reasons for their apparently strange decisions. The refusal of the administrator of AIR to forward my scholarship application was one of these strange acts. What else can I say? Sometimes it is very difficult to understand human behavior and motivation. It is mysterious indeed.

The next week, the results of MA examination were announced. I not only secured a first class, but also was top-ranked among all Economics students in my college. The college principal personally called and congratulated me. The University of Delhi immediately sent me an invitation to become a tutor for BA honors students. Hansraj College, an affiliated college of Delhi University, offered me a lectureship in Economics, and asked me to join within two weeks.

Within the next two days, another surprise awaited me. I was offered an appointment by the Ministry of Home Affairs as a result of the UPSC selection examination I had completed several months before. Now I was in a quandary, once again.

Two compelling employment offers, both very interesting, with good future prospects! Should I become an economics lecturer or an officer in the Indian Ministerial Services? I faced a true dilemma. I would have to make a choice soon.

When one is offered two job opportunities, one of the foremost considerations is salary. I believe the government job offer would have started with an initial salary of Rs.400 vis-à-vis the teaching job, paying about Rs.450.

The former job would have provided many opportunities for promotion and advancement in the various administrative services of the government of India. The latter would have given good salary increases, commensurate with one's performance and abilities.

The ministry job was considered prestigious and permanent. One of the major considerations in choosing a job, especially in India, would have been the likelihood of its permanence. A central government job was universally considered very desirable in those days. On the other hand, private enterprise jobs as well as most academic positions were not considered "permanent," and therefore did not compare favorably with government jobs. Job security was thought to be of paramount importance in the minds of most Indian job seekers. Good government jobs were eagerly snapped up by most candidates who were offered them.

The teaching job offered to me was purely temporary. It was good only for the first year, with the prospect for renewal subject to satisfactory performance as a lecturer. There was absolutely no guarantee that it would be renewed the following year.

Most job seekers in India, I think, did not give too much importance or weight to one's true inner calling or professional interests. Good current salary, prestige, job security and prospects for promotion were the major considerations in selecting a job. In those days, almost all job applicants were looking for these characteristics in their employment search. In the India I grew up in and knew, teaching in a college or university was not considered as lucrative, prestigious or desirable as an officer's position in the Central Secretariat Service.

Thus, the choices I faced at that time made me search my soul very carefully. I was somewhat of a rebel in almost everything I did in my life. I had learned several hard lessons during the ten years since I left Vilayur. I had gone through some memorable experiences and personal situations, which made me strong in my mind and will power. Most of the decision-making situations I had faced hitherto taught me to trust my instincts. In the ultimate analysis, one has to live with the consequences of the decisions one makes, and not depend on others to tell us what to do. It is a truism that no one else knows our own minds as well as we do. I knew that my own personal interests, abilities and determination should guide me in what I chose and what I did.

I had no experience in teaching. I did not know what to expect in an academic teaching job. Perhaps I might turn out to be a failure as a college lecturer. The students may be too difficult to handle and control. Delhi University students were notorious for their rowdy, undisciplined behavior in the classroom. Lecturing them would not be easy. Could I control a big class? If I chose the teaching profession, would my future turn out to be as bright financially and professionally as the government job? Teaching was absolutely unchartered territory for me. I had known and seen good and bad teachers. Would I be a successful teacher? These considerations weighed heavily on my mind.

Another minor but not insignificant consideration was this: While the government job would have been a continuation of my prior five years of service in government employment at AIR, the teaching job would constitute a complete breach from my current post.

I think most of my friends and well wishers advised me to take the secretariat job. Is that what I truly wanted for myself? Should I follow their advice? I pondered the choice before me night and day for the next several days. I decided to follow my gut instincts and make a clean sweep.

I made up my mind to quit my present job and accept the lectureship immediately. I notified AIR of my decision.

With a racing heart and full of trepidation, I showed up at Hansraj College the following day. I was assigned to teach Basic Economics and Japanese Economic History courses. I plunged into my assignments with a lot of anxiety. It was not easy for me to ascend the podium on the first day of class. The initial and second class meetings did not go well. Although I had prepared for the class thoroughly and knew my subject matter well, my lack of experience and hesitation in front of the students must have been transparent. Some of them jeered, some made big noises from the back benches (seats) and some discreetly passed around slips of paper (probably with many jokes scribbled about me) among themselves. I knew they were determined to test my mettle and disrupt my lecture. I tried to teach pretending that nothing was happening, not showing any signs of my sweaty palms and trembling feet. To my great relief, the bell rang; the class period ended, and I began to wonder whether I was indeed cut out to be a teacher. Did I make a blunder in leaving the previous job and taking up this one?

I knew there was nothing to do but try to make the best possible effort. The next day, I told the students that they should give me a fair chance to teach them, and judge my teaching skills alone—not my disciplinary abilities. I told them that until yesterday I too was a student, just like all of them; that I became a lecturer purely on the basis of my knowledge and proficiency in the subject. Most of them listened, thank God, and sat politely through the class. In a few days, I gained poise, experience and control of the class. There were still a few rowdy students in the back benches determined to disrupt the class, but I continued to ignore them. Most of the students remained genuinely interested. I believe my command of the subject and ability to explain the concepts I was teaching must have impressed most of the students as genuine scholarship. My sincerity and enthusiasm must have gained their respect.

My new job continued for the next three months. I became more and more confident of my ability as a teacher as I learned to adapt to my newfound responsibility. I slowly began to enjoy my role as a budding developer of young minds and moved with increasing confidence among my teaching colleagues. I was determined to do my very best in my new job and make a success of it. There was no going back for me.

Within a few weeks, an advertisement appeared in the Delhi newspapers announcing a teaching position in Economics at the newly opened SV College on Rouse Avenue. This proved a golden opportunity for me to get a more permanent position. I applied, and was selected. I requested the head of the Economics Department at Hansraj College to relieve me from my job, which he readily did. I joined SV College in August 1961 and continued there as Lecturer in Economics until August 1963. When I started, my salary was almost 500 rupees, and during the next year I got an increment, raising it to almost 600 rupees.

In retrospect, I was vindicated. I had made the right move in choosing teaching as my profession. Soon, I became very successful in my job, and was indeed popular with the student body. It did not take me long to earn the professional respect of my faculty colleagues too.

My work experience has taught me that one is fortunate to choose a calling that combines a decent income as well as love for what one does to make a living. This is a rare blessing indeed. Those who are able to combine both of these characteristics in a job are truly fortunate. To be able to spend most of the working hours of one's day in doing something we enjoy is one of life's true pleasures! Hoorah.

# Chapter 8

## Family Responsibilities

For almost ten years, since I began working in Hyderabad, I was regularly sending money to my parents. I knew from my childhood experiences the extreme financial hardships they had endured in raising a large family. My mother had given birth to twelve children from 1929 to 1954. I was their third child.

My father's monthly salary was totally insufficient for meeting even our basic household expenses. I knew, without being told, how hard up he was. The financial situation at home was still desperate, even though four children had left home. My elder brother Mani was a high school teacher in Palghat. My sister Thylam had been married and left home in 1954. My younger brother Ramakrishnan had joined me in Hyderabad in 1956.

I had considered it my solemn responsibility to remit home as much money as I could to help my parents. I knew they were dependent on Ramakrishnan and me for financial support. We pooled our resources together. It gave me great pleasure and relief to know that we could help our parents financially as much as we did. My younger siblings did not face as much hardship and deprivation as I did during my own childhood, even though their daily life was not materially much better. It was simply hard for my parents, with their meager resources, to raise a large family. Every time I visited home during vacation or holidays I could see for myself that, in spite of our regular financial contributions, my parents still could not afford a more desirable lifestyle. Their daily toil and hardship continued for many more years.

I was especially concerned with my mother's condition. She had been toiling from dawn to dusk every day of her adult life. She had very little by way of material comforts. The necessity to take care of her children's needs constantly kept her busy with cooking, cleaning, washing and doing dozens of household chores. She did

67

not have any respite from the repeated drudgery of housework. I was acutely aware of her burden and felt much distressed by it, but could not personally help her much. The only thing I could do was to share my income with the family so as to ease their financial hardship somewhat. I did this cheerfully, with complete awareness of my filial responsibility.

Since my childhood I had learned to look up to my mother as the embodiment of goodness. She was simplicity incarnate. Her dedication to the family was total. Although she worked so hard, she seldom complained about her lot in life. She led a simple life. Her greatest strengths were acceptance of her physical environment, faith in God, sincerity, serenity and love of family.

I considered it incumbent on my part to share my income with my parents to make their financial life a little easier. After meeting my own living and educational expenses as well as regular remittances to the family, there was very little left from my paycheck to save. Although I had opened a savings account at the post office, it grew very slowly over those years. The only real luxury I indulged in was to enroll in the gliding classes at Safdarjung Airport in Delhi. I had taken a fascination for gliding. The exhilaration of floating high up in the glider was very thrilling. But after a few months, I abandoned gliding because I found it to be a heavy drain on the budget.

In the summer of 1962, my mother was invited by her brother Krishnamurti in Bangalore to visit him. This was probably the only long vacation she had known in many years. My brother Ananthan escorted her. She spent a few happy days in Bangalore, and asked me to join her there. I was overjoyed to do this. It gave me an opportunity to visit Bangalore after almost ten years and get acquainted with my uncle's family. After consulting with him, I decided to take my mother on a side trip to Mysore to see the beautiful Brindavan Gardens. We had a grand time and I was very happy to spend a few days with her there. Thereafter, we all returned to Vilayur.

Soon afterward, my parents sent my younger brother Vaitha to join Ramakrishnan and me in New Delhi. Within a few weeks of his arrival, Vaitha obtained a job. He was extremely smart, hardworking and learned to adapt to his new urban environment with ease. Our personal supervision, coaching and guidance probably helped him to adapt and thrive in New Delhi in record time.

By now I had completed my twenty-fifth birthday. I had been living independently for almost ten years. During this period, I was recording some of my life's lessons and philosophy in a diary. Since leaving Vilayur, I had been reading, studying, observing and experiencing a lot of different things. I found it worthwhile to write about them and visualize my own mental development and maturity. The idea that other family members may benefit from my recorded thoughts was also a driving force in doing this. Making decisions affecting my life, earning a living, spending wisely, and being master of my fate since the age of sixteen had given me important insights about how to conduct one's life. My friends used to jokingly call me a "philosopher in the making."

# Chapter 9

## Romance in the Air

After joining SV College, my daily routine had become somewhat stable and less hectic compared to the preceding years. Teaching my classes became second nature. Without too much conscious effort, I was able to discharge my academic duties. I enjoyed my teaching job and the freedom it gave me to do whatever I wanted. There was no need to sit in an office eight hours a day, as had been the case previously. My students were mostly docile, and I had complete command over the classroom. It was hard to believe that only a few months before, controlling the classroom environment had presented a formidable challenge.

Observing my close camaraderie with the students, the college principal appointed me as faculty advisor to the students union. I started planning and directing various cultural events. One of these was our college's participation in the Delhi University Youth Festival. Student teams were chosen through competition to represent our college in different programs such as art, music, dance and debating. Some of my colleagues were in charge of different events, while I took charge of the student music team.

When my second academic year at SV College began in July 1962, there was a new batch of entering students with great talent in music and the arts. Among them was Kamala. She was also enrolled in my basic economics class. She was sitting along with her friends in the classroom in one corner. She seemed to me like a beautiful rose bud about to open its petals. She had a very pleasing smile on her face and beamed constantly. I was immediately attracted to her personality and used to steal glances at her while she was engaged in taking notes in the class, if only half seriously.

Early one morning she came to my faculty desk along with her friends and asked some questions. I was happy to answer them. In general, most of the students in my classes were silent most of the

71

time. Very few would ask questions or come to me outside of the classroom for extra help. Kamala was different. She seemed bold, and with her smiling face always spoke as if she was the leader of the group. The female students always came in a group. I wanted to speak to Kamala individually. I was waiting for an opportunity to do this.

One day, after a long time, I saw her walking alone. Approaching her, I greeted her. After some preliminary conversation and pleasantries, I asked if she would like to accompany me to a Circarama Show in town. The show had come to Delhi a few weeks earlier. I had been thinking of seeing it. She politely refused the sudden, and I suppose, unexpected invitation.

I was relieved that the ice was broken. At last we had talked, without being observed by other students.

After several days of glancing surreptitiously at each other in the classroom, I was looking for an opportunity to talk to her again. It was very hard to do this, because she was always in the company of other female friends. The atmosphere in the college was not conducive to meeting her individually. There were always crowds of people everywhere.

Another day I noticed that she was getting into a bus to go home after class. I too boarded that bus and greeted her. We chatted about inconsequential things, and I told her we needed to talk to each other soon. I assumed that she knew why. She agreed to find a suitable time and place, and went her way. We had made the initial contact, and I was eagerly waiting for the next meeting.

One afternoon, we got into the bus together. We sat next to each other, and conversed. Soon the bus reached Sujan Singh Park, near her home. She said it was time for her to get down. I too got out along with her and we walked together for a few yards. Soon I had to leave her. We agreed to see each other again as soon as possible.

Gradually, those afternoon bus trips after class became more frequent. We would alight at Sujan Singh Park and walk toward

72

Lodhi Gardens instead of her home. Perhaps for an hour, we would wander in the gardens, delighting in each other's company. After some days, we started going together to Connaught Place. Our favorite meeting place was the Volga Restaurant. We had to be very careful not to be observed by anyone we knew. To be seen in public together would have spelled disaster for us. We had to be discreet and extremely secretive.

Many times, when other students were in the bus going in our direction, either I would get out before reaching Sujan Singh Park and walk fast toward the next bus stop, or go past her bus stop, then alight, and run toward her. It was indeed a desperate game. We could not be seen in public together. It would have been scandalous. Rumors would spread, and our reputations might get tarnished. We could not allow that to happen. It would have also been the end of our budding romance.

Within a few months, we grew close. We liked each other very much. Our conversations were very enjoyable. This was undoubtedly "love," I thought. We cherished our time together. On a few occasions, which were rare, we managed to get away from the familiar beaten paths in the city. Once or twice, we found time to wander in the far away Buddha Jayanthi Park and among the gardens in Okhla.

The most memorable day in our lives happened one late afternoon in the spacious, beautiful gardens around Humayun's Tomb. We had talked the previous day, and decided that we wanted to be free from the fear of being observed by anyone. We took a long bus ride and got out near Humayun's Tomb. It was a glorious, bright, sunny day. The rose bushes in the surrounding gardens were in full bloom. We wandered around the flowers, and for the first time I emboldened myself to hold Kamala's hands. The experience was electrifying. We could not hold back our emotions. We walked hand in hand, and talked for a long time. It was soon time to go home, as the day was getting late. On our way out, we both agreed that we should continue our lives together forever. I think both of us then became conscious of our growing feelings of love for each other.

The question was, how could we pull this off? The social and practical obstacles in our way were formidable.

One of the basic difficulties in our being together was our respective positions in the social hierarchy. I was a teacher, and she was my student. The world frowned upon romantic relations between teacher and student. No matter. I knew that social ostracism had not prevented other student-teacher pairs from becoming lovers. We had to keep our feelings for each other completely secret from everybody. This was a challenging task, which we met squarely. Obviously there was no place in the college environment for any conversations between us, other than academic ones. In fact, we managed to keep our distance without giving anybody any suspicion of our longing for each other. The proper decorum and etiquette expected between a teacher and student were observed by both of us on the college campus.

But this was not enough. It was absolutely essential that other teachers, students, college officials and people known to us should not see us going out together. In the eyes of the world, we had no business being together by ourselves. Society would not look kindly upon an unmarried pair like us being alone together. We were very conscious of the fact that one of Kamala's father's associates (or a relative) may somehow discover her in the company of an adult male (stranger) and report it to her parents. Such an event would have been disastrous for her reputation. That would have spelled the end of our budding romance. In the 1960s, the then-prevalent social mores, moral strictures and norms of appropriate behavior between unmarried members of the opposite sex did not permit talking to each other—except in the company of family and friends. For a man and woman to go out together, unescorted or chaperoned, was almost unthinkable. The woman's reputation would be tarnished forever, and her family would be unable to bear the associated social stigma. Society simply did not permit us to be seen together, alone, in public, unless we were already married. The reader will no doubt find it very hard to appreciate from the vantage point of today how 'conservative' our society was when Kamala and I were "dating" each other. Very hard, indeed!

Kamala was barely eighteen years old then. I was about twenty-seven. At that time, her parents were making preparations for the marriage of their second daughter, Usha. The marriage was to take place in July 1963. The family belonged to an orthodox, upper middle class Iyengar community. Kamala's parents were extremely conservative. Her father, CRG, was an administrative officer in the Ministry of Finance. Her brothers, Kasturi and Ramu, were in high school. At home, they spoke their native language, Tamil. Her mother, Saroja, doted on Kamala, her third and youngest daughter.

I was born and brought up in rural Kerala. My ancestors belonged to the "Iyer" community. Our native language was Malayalam, not Tamil. Kamala and I had conversed in English ever since we met. We did not really know each other's language well enough to converse. My parents were also extremely traditional in their outlook. It was doubtful if they would entertain a proposal of marriage between our two sects. Even though both Iyengars and Iyers were upper class Brahmins in the Indian caste structure, intermarriage between the two communities was uncommon—indeed, very rare. Their respective religious beliefs, social customs and conventions were very different from each other. Members of the two communities simply did not marry each other. That would have been considered heresy. The question of our bringing up the subject of our marriage before our respective parents was, of course, out of the question. So, in the normal course of things, our romantic relationship would not have culminated in a conventional marriage with parental or social blessings.

We did not, of course, pay much attention to these mundane considerations. Indeed, we did not talk about getting married until several months later, when unexpected future events forced us to do so. Until then, we were simply happy to be in each other's company whenever we could, although those opportunities did not occur often enough.

Getting together with each other became harder and harder as the weeks rolled by. It seemed to us, or so we imagined, that the eyes of everyone were watching us all the time. We had no opportunity to talk, let alone go out together alone, unobserved. If, by chance, we happened to cross each other in the halls, we tended not to look at each other for too long. All I could get was a furtive glance or two from my beloved. It was getting to be sheer torture, to say the least. Although I could see Kamala in my class twice or thrice a week, I could not converse with her. This was an unusual situation. "So near, and yet so far!" Those favorite words of Nehru rang true in my ears all the time.

In December 1962, I had to escort our college's music team to the Delhi University's Annual Youth Festival. As faculty advisor, I was in charge of making arrangements to transport our college student team to the university campus, and later take them back home. Kamala was one of the participants in the music team. Along with four of her friends, I escorted the team to the festival. After completion of the event, I brought them back and dropped each student at his or her respective home, keeping my sweetheart till the end. At last, we got a chance to hold hands and have a brief conversation. After a few minutes, I had to say goodbye and drop Kamala in front of her house. It was hard to know when we would get another chance to be together again! We had to be especially careful not to be seen by the world in each other's company. The price of proximity would have been too high. Such is the course of "true love," as we are reminded by Shakespeare.

Now I must take a respite from these romantic ruminations, and resume the narration of my academic aspirations.

Although I greatly enjoyed teaching at SV College, I continued my constant pursuit of avenues for higher studies abroad. There was a strong desire in me to do a Ph.D. degree in Economics. Looking through the USIS Library, I came across several American university catalogs outlining their Ph.D. programs. After choosing some of these randomly, I applied for admission, along with requests for scholarships, assistantships and financial aid.

Almost all American universities start their academic years in the fall, i.e., September of each other. When I applied, it was January 1963. By April, I got a few rejections letters as well as some acceptance letters. The universities that sent acceptance letters indicated that they could not provide financial assistance during the first academic year. Without financial help, I could not afford to go abroad. I was getting somewhat disappointed.

Then, all of a sudden, I heard from Wayne State University in Detroit, Michigan. It was indeed welcome news. They admitted me into their Ph.D. program, with a teaching assistantship for the first year. If I performed well, the assistantship would be extended in the subsequent years. The initial stipend for nine months would be $1,900, with the possibility of an additional small summer stipend. They informed me that I should communicate my acceptance of the offer immediately if I wanted to join in September 1963, as another standby was waiting for my place should I choose not to go. They could not provide any travel assistance, and I would have to make the trip to America on my own.

Once again, I found myself at a crossroads. What was I to do? I had very little money saved up to make the trip. That would require several thousands of rupees. Other important considerations weighed on me too. What would happen to my budding romance? Could I leave my sweetheart Kamala and go alone, without her by my side, for a possible three-year study program? If I left her behind, what would happen to her? Did I really possess the requisite mathematical/statistical skills to enter a Ph.D. program and succeed in it? Could I cope with living in a foreign country and get used to the American way of life?

Previous dilemmas I had faced danced in my mind. In a sense, this was no different, although there were more difficult questions now that needed answers. Pondering over the matter, I sought additional information wherever I could find it. I talked to a couple of people I knew. I went to Delhi University Library and searched for additional data.

I knew that somehow I would succeed in solving the financial problem in due course. Even though I was unable to raise funds immediately to pay for the trip, there was still time until September. I could explore various ways of dealing with it more leisurely.

Surely, I did not want to forego a good opportunity like this for lack of money.

I reasoned that my misgivings about my mathematics background required for a Ph.D. program were probably unwarranted. Why not give it a try and put myself through the test? I would have to learn the requisite mathematical skills. If I failed, I would have to live with its consequences. So what? Life is a matter of learning through trial and error.

The questions of lifestyle changes and adjustments or adaptation to America were not insoluble either. When we are thrown in a new, unfamiliar environment, we instinctively learn to survive and thrive in it. There is no other way. Had I not learned these lessons well through personal, firsthand experience? Born and brought up in rural Kerala, had I not met the challenge of living in unfamiliar urban settings? Did I not succeed and prosper in Hyderabad and New Delhi? Surely I could do much better in America if I set my mind to it.

These problems paled in insignificance in comparison with another, much closer to my heart. The most intractable question, it seemed, was my future life with Kamala. How could I deal with our separation? What would Kamala do in my absence? In the event of a traditional marriage proposal for her coming up while I was away, how would she deal with it? Could our love survive my absence without nurture? If we could not easily communicate with each other when we were both in Delhi, how could we do this separated by the oceans? What was the solution? I found myself without any clue. The only thing to do was to discuss everything with Kamala, ask for her opinion, and then decide.

The question and its answer were soon dealt with. As if through telepathy, student Kamala came to her teacher's desk seeking an answer to one of the questions in her economics course.

Thereupon, I urged on her the necessity of a meeting to resolve an urgent problem of my own. I told her we must get together the next day if her mother would grant her permission to return home late after class. As she was the president of the Fine Arts Society, this would be a legitimate excuse.

We went to the Volga Restaurant for a long conversation. I knew that our whole future was at stake. Kamala was itching to know why I had invited her for a sudden "urgent" discussion, and eager to find out what it was all about. We had a cup of tea, and then the ensuing conversation began:

Gopal: "I have something very important to tell you. It needs a lot of discussion. That is why we came here."

Kamala: "What is it? Is it something about me?"

Gopal: "Yes, of course. It is about both of us. I mean, our future life together. Shall I tell you?"

Kamala: "Go ahead. Please tell me."

Gopal: "I have obtained a scholarship to study in the United States. I want to go for a Ph.D. Usually a Ph.D. program requires three or four years. I do not know whether I should go or not. What do you think?"

Kamala: "Of course you should go. It is a great opportunity. I am so glad. When do you have to go?"

Gopal: "They want me to join in September. Usually all classes start in September, and the university suggests that foreign students should arrive at week or two earlier to get used to the place. So, if I decide to go, I must do so in August, probably the third week or so."

Kamala: "Have you made any arrangements?"

Gopal: "How can I? Without consulting my beloved? Of course not. I wanted to tell you first. What should I do? I want your frank opinion."

Kamala: "I know you will do very well. A Ph.D. will enhance your future prospects so much. Why do you hesitate? What is the problem?"

Gopal: "The problem is our future. If I decide to go, what will happen to you? I may not be able to return until I finish my studies.

79

Once I go, it is very difficult to come back. It is hard to predict when I will finish. Therefore, I am hesitant to go, leaving you alone. What will happen to you? What shall we do about our separation for such a long time?"

Kamala: "I will manage. I will continue my studies. I will follow your example and go for higher studies myself. Perhaps I will go for a master's degree. In fact, my father was talking the other day that I should get a master's degree."

Gopal: "That is very good. I am glad you want to study. I too want you to study, no question about that. But I was thinking about our future together. I am afraid that your parents will hitch you to somebody when I am gone. You will get married. I cannot live without you."

Kamala: "I too am thinking about us. I do not think I will marry anybody else but you. My father cannot afford to get me married after he has spent all that money on Usha's coming marriage. He is already in deep debt. He is borrowing so much to get her married. At least I don't think he will marry me off soon. So you needn't worry on my score."

Gopal: "You never know. Suppose some marriage proposal comes up. Suppose somebody comes up with a good proposal and your parents agree to that. What are you going to do?"

Kamala: "Don't worry. I will refuse. I will not entertain any marriage proposal. I will wait for you. I won't marry anybody except you. I cannot live without you."

Gopal: "I know you do. But things can change. Circumstances can change. I am afraid that something bad, something we cannot foresee today, may happen to frustrate our future plans. Something like that always happens. I have seen too many cases where parents have forced their daughter to marry somebody they chose. They don't bother about what you think. They will force you to marry, and that is all. There is nothing you can about it."

Kamala: "I don't think so. You don't know me. I will wait for you. If it comes to that, I will tell my parents that I have already promised you to marry only you. You can depend on me. But I too am worried that I will be unable to bear our separation. Already I am pining for you every day. Whenever I see you in college and can't talk to you or go out with you, I can't bear it. I don't know what I will do without you for three years."

Gopal: "Precisely. That is what I was thinking, too. We are here and see each other in college, but can't talk to each other. Our respective situations as teacher and student prevent us from getting together. That is not going to change for at least two more years, until you complete your BA. Only after that can we be together always, without worrying about the world."

Kamala: "So, I will wait for one more year, until you come back."

Gopal: "But I can't predict that I will be able to finish my Ph.D. in three years. What if I can't return in three years? What shall we do then? Suppose it takes longer, what then?"

Kamala: "You can finish. You are smart. I know you will finish soon."

Gopal: "You give me too much credit. That is very nice of you. But we have to plan for unexpected contingencies. I don't think we can predict what will happen. We must have a plan of action, just in case."

Kamala: "I know what you mean. Then what do you suggest?"

Gopal: "I think it is a gamble. I don't want to lose you. I have too much invested in you emotionally. I cannot give you up. I think I will decide not to go, that is all."

Kamala: "No, no. Don't do that. I will never be able to live with that. You are so bright. You are so smart. You shouldn't give up an opportunity like this. Not everyone gets a chance to go to the USA to do a Ph.D. I know so many of my father's relatives who are in America. You should not sacrifice your whole future."

Gopal: "I know. I am thinking of a possible solution. Can we get married before I leave? That would solve our problems. If we are married, nobody can take you away from me. Nobody ever. Then our future will be secure. We will have each other forever."

Kamala: "How can we marry? My parents would never permit that, I know. They are too orthodox, too conservative. They will throw me out. Besides, how can we marry now? How are we going to arrange all that in such a short time?"

Gopal: "I am just thinking. What if we get married in secret? A civil marriage? Do you know what that means? Have you ever heard of such a thing?"

Kamala: "Yes, I have. That is somebody marrying in a court, in front of a judge. Can we do that? Tell me more."

Gopal: "I don't know exactly how it is done. I have heard that some people do it when they are desperate, or when their parents do not permit them to get married in the conventional way. It depends on what they want to do, how much they love each other. We can inquire. I will find out the procedure. Are you willing to do that if I find out? Will you be willing to go with me to the court and get married without your parents knowing about it? It is very risky."

Kamala: "I have already decided that I will only marry you or none at all. I want you as much as you want me. Why do you doubt my resolve? I will do anything for you. I love you. Tell me what to do, and I will do it."

Gopal: "You are brave. You are so good. I admire your courage. I think we should definitely get married before I go. Then I can go in peace. Then I can concentrate on my studies without thinking about you all the time. Once you are mine, no one can separate us. Once we are married, and have proof of it, our future together is secure. I think that is the only way out of our dilemma. I can go abroad and do my studies. I can have you as my wife. I do not have to worry about our future. As soon as I can, I will sponsor you, and you can join me in America."

Kamala: "Then you please find out the details. College will close in two or three weeks. We have no time to lose. We will have to do everything fast. I think you yourself will have to do whatever needs to be done. I cannot be of any help."

Gopal: "All right. I will find out the procedure. I will let you know. Are you sure you want to get married like this, without telling your parents? What a brave girl!"

Kamala: "I too think that this is the only way to ensure our future together. Once we are married on paper, I can tell my parents about it when the time comes. They will understand then. I will explain to them why I did it. Circumstances are such that we have no other way to ensure our happiness. Are you going to tell your parents?"

Gopal: "Of course not. My parents are not going to approve of my marrying like this. They are just like your parents. They are old fashioned. They want me to get married in a traditional way, I am sure. Perhaps they are right now considering various proposals from prospective girls."

Kamala: "I know. We are both in the same boat. I am glad I got to know you. We have so much in common. I wouldn't want to get married like my sisters, Prema or Usha. I am lucky to have known you. You are so different from anybody I have seen."

Gopal: "Yes, we are both very fortunate, darling. Love is the greatest force in the world. To love someone with all one's heart is the greatest blessing in life. We have each other. It is a precious gift. I thank God for finding you. I love you so much. You have made me whole. Before you came into my life, it was so dull and boring. Now I am fully alive. I go to the college looking for a glimpse of you. I am so glad I found you. You are my life."

Kamala: "It is getting late. My mother will be expecting me. I told her I would be home by five o'clock. I think we should go now."

Gopal: "All right. So you agree that we should get married through a civil ceremony? Are you sure that is what you want to do? Remember that once we sign the papers, there is no going back. You are stuck with me for good!"

Kamala: "Don't tease me like that. You know I want it. We have agreed upon our plan of action. There is no other way. I am serious. Let us do it. I will wait for you to tell me what to do."

Gopal: "Thank you, darling. I love you so much. I live for you. I will get the information, and we shall do what we have to do. Now I will take you home."

With a heavy heart and full of thoughts about the unknown future, we took a taxi to Kamala's house.

# Chapter 10

## Overcoming New Obstacles

The agenda before me was daunting. I made a mental note of the tasks to be accomplished:

Obtain an application form for my passport, and submit it soon.

Find out the procedure for a civil marriage. Obtain the necessary filing papers, and file the petition as required by law.

Send a "thank you" acceptance letter to Wayne State University.

Pursue fund-raising efforts to finance my forthcoming trip to the United States.

The easiest of these to do was item number three, so I did that immediately.

Then I started a methodical follow-up of the other tasks one by one—nay, simultaneously. There was no time to be lost.

Obtaining a passport turned out to be much harder than I had imagined. I assumed that all I had to do was simply obtain an application form, fill it out, and file it along with the requisite fee. My assumption, though logical, turned out to be wrong. The next few weeks turned out to be some of the most harrowing and stressful in my life. It is hard to imagine that such a simple thing as obtaining a passport can turn out to be such a difficult task! I learned through first-hand experience the truth of the adage, "It is whom you know that matters."

Filling out the passport application was no doubt very easy. But the application had to be countersigned (attested) by a "Gazetted Officer," or a person of comparable rank in the bureaucracy. Traditionally, the Indian bureaucratic machine had set a great deal of store in its Gazetted Officers cadre, who commanded a good deal of power and prestige in social circles.

To get the passport, a statement was required from a Gazetted Officer certifying that he/she knew the applicant personally for several years. This requirement almost amounted to an implicit guarantee, vouching for the character and conduct of the applicant.

Unfortunately, I knew no such Gazetted Officer. The irony of the situation was that none of the people I happened to know well were eligible to sign the required statement. Most unexpectedly, I thus found myself up against a bureaucratic wall. Still I did talk to a couple of Gazetted Officers, whom I thought I knew, hoping to persuade one of them to sign the required certification. My attempts were completely unsuccessful. My pleading with them and reasoning that this would cause them no harm or trouble fell on deaf ears. I was then reminded of my previous failed attempt to persuade the administrative officer of AIR to forward my Commonwealth Scholarship application.

Absolutely frustrated by the attitude of these Gazetted Officers, I was now at a loss to understand what to do next. Was I going to give up my pursuit of higher education abroad just because I could not obtain a passport? And the sole reason for this new predicament—because I did not happen to know a Gazetted Officer well enough? My sterling character, my burning ambition, my proven academic record, my good intentions and my varied accomplishments so far—all these were of no consequence? Were these not worthy of the signature of a Gazetted Officer? I couldn't believe what was happening to me. For a moment at least I was completely paralyzed by negative thinking.

These thoughts kept roiling in my brain. I lay awake, seething with anger and disbelief at my pitiable situation. I could not get sleep. I cried, but not for too long. Then, all of a sudden, I got an idea.

Why not send a letter to my uncle, Mr. Krishnamurti, who was then Director of the Central Water and Power Commission in Simla, bringing my plight to his attention? Surely he would understand my predicament and help me, I reasoned. I wrote him a letter immediately, and hoped he would come to my rescue.

86

Sure enough, within a few days, my uncle invited me to meet him. On the very next day, I boarded the train to Simla. At last, I managed to obtain the most coveted Gazetted Officer endorsement on my passport application. Once again, I learned the lesson that persistence and determination pays, and that one should not give up on a problem until a solution can be found. The passport was obtained a few weeks thereafter. Subsequently, I also got the necessary F1 Student Visa from the American Embassy. One more hurdle was now crossed.

* * *

FOOTNOTE: Some rules are almost always arbitrary. Sometimes they do change over time, when regimes change. I am happy to report that the archaic and unnecessarily restrictive/cumbersome requirements for obtaining an Indian passport are now history. Nowadays any decent citizen of India is automatically entitled to obtain a passport, without having to know a Gazetted Officer. Passport procedures have been greatly simplified.

* * *

While pursuing the passport episode, I was also engaged in finding the requisite funding for my trip abroad. My plan of action was to:

Request from some of my friends an outright gift or loan, to the extent of their financial abilities.

Plead my case to Swami Ranganathananda of the Ramakrishna Mission, whom I knew personally. I hoped the swami was in a position to help.

Ask various family members for contributions, to the best of their abilities and resources.

Meet and discuss my case with the President of the Congress for Cultural Freedom.

Apply for a travel grant from a charitable or educational foundation.

While searching for travel funds to finance my trip, an earlier conversation with my Uncle Ponnanna came to my mind. He had told me, "Those who want to help you usually do not have the means; those who have the means do not usually help you."

Those words had always struck a chord in my mind. I discovered, through experience once again, the partial truth of this statement. Nevertheless, my relentless search for money continued, and I was not willing to give up easily.

I went to the Delhi Public Library and looked for directories listing various sources of travel money. Many of these sources needed lengthy applications and a lot of time to process. Rather than pursue those potential donors, I decided to tap a few selected sources I knew personally. In a couple of months, I collected the tidy sum of almost five thousand rupees. The major contributions came from the following:

A couple of friends gave me gifts of Rs.400.

Swami R donated Rs.200.

My brothers Ramakrishnan and Vaitha contributed Rs.1,000.

The President of the Congress for Cultural Freedom put me in touch with a top official in the Ministry of Commerce, Mr. Majumdar, who gave me an introductory letter to meet Lala Charat Ram, Chairman of the Delhi Cloth Mills. Accordingly, I got an appointment to meet him, and explained my need for travel funds. After listening patiently to my request, Lala Charat Ram promised to extend an interest-free loan of Rs.2,000, to be repaid at a future time, whenever I chose to do so. I was overjoyed by this generous gesture. Lala Charat Ram did not want any loan documents to be signed. It was understood between us that I would honor his implicit trust in me. I thanked him profusely for his kindness and timely help.

* * *

FOOTNOTE: About five years later, soon after I obtained a job in the United States, I repaid the loan. Lala Charat Ram's generosity had taken care of the lion's share of my travel budget.

Another source I had been tapping for travel funds told me that occasionally, the President of India might consider such requests based on merit. Accordingly, I decided to meet the President of India, Dr. Radhakrishnan. On the appointed day, I went to the Mughal Gardens in Rashtrapathi Bhavan, where the president was receiving people who had come to meet him. I stood in line for a long time, almost two hours. After greeting each person, the president would listen patiently to his or her plea. At last, it was my turn. Within a few minutes of our meeting, the president informed me that he would issue instructions to his private secretary to help me in whatever way was possible. I bowed before him, and thanked him for his kind words.

When I went to the president's office later, I was told that he had authorized to give me a travel grant of Rs.1,000.

With this grant, almost all of the money I needed for travel was either at hand, or was promised when needed.

Having raised the requisite travel money, I was now eager to turn my energies to the other important task ahead of me: the marriage petition.

# Chapter 11

## A Clandestine Marriage

Soon after our conversation at Volga Restaurant regarding the decision to get married secretly, I went to the Delhi District Court to find out the procedure for a civil marriage. The steps needed were simple. We were required to sign a petition/declaration of the proposed marriage, and post a notice in the marriage court for thirty days. Such a notice was also required to be published in a local newspaper. This was supposed to provide an opportunity for any interested party in the matter to comment. This requirement frightened me somewhat. What if somebody known to either of us saw the notice and discovered our secret plan! We had to provide some basic personal information about ourselves, along with a nominal filing fee. After the waiting period was completed, we could appear before the marriage officer and solemnize our marriage.

Fortunately, only one of the parties to the proposed marriage had to go to court personally to submit the petition. The other party could affix his or her signature to the petition.

I picked up the requisite application form. The task before me now was to obtain Kamala's signature on the petition. My departure to the United States was tentatively scheduled for late August. Therefore, it was imperative that we should submit the marriage petition without delay. College had already closed for the summer vacation. We could not afford to wait until reopening day; that would have been too late.

Earlier, Kamala and I had reached an understanding that she would telephone me whenever she could during the two-month duration of the summer vacation. I could neither telephone nor write to her during that period. I was anxiously waiting for her call.

One day, the expected call came. I then informed Kamala that we should soon get together somewhere for her signature on the petition. She agreed she would try to meet me at the British Council Library on June 2, after lunch. On that day, I waited for her with trepidation, walking back and forth like a caged lion in the library corridors.

After a while she arrived, with books in her arms, accompanied by her younger brother, Ramu. I greeted Ramu after being introduced by Kamala. She informed me that her mother had sent Ramu along for good company. We wandered in the library for a while. In a few minutes, both of us managed to disappear behind the bookshelves under the pretext of looking for some book. I hastily pulled the petition from my pocket, and Kamala affixed her signature on it.

There are certain moments in our lives when we cannot find words to express the depth of our emotions and feelings. I found myself at such a moment on that occasion.

Though we had planned this strategy and knew that there was no other way to execute our marriage plan, the seriousness of the step we had just taken was awesome. Kamala's courage and determination were remarkable. I couldn't but admire what she had just done. After all, I was a man, supposedly well versed in the affairs of the world. I was certainly older, and probably wiser, according to the proverbs. Here was an innocent, young woman who had come from the home of her doting parents, prepared to tie up her whole future life with me, with absolute trust in the outcome. I was overwhelmed. To commit oneself for life to another person, purely on the strength of mutual love and trust, required absolute certainty about the other. I realized then what my responsibility toward her was, and I steeled myself to meet it. To say that I resolved myself to be worthy of such love and trust is hardly sufficient. I had always taken pride in my absolute sincerity, steadfastness and sense of purpose. No doubt, from the outset I was resolute in my solemn commitment and devotion to Kamala. At the same time, her unqualified, unreserved devotion to me, and dedication to our future life together, was sheer ecstasy. We were indeed meant for each other, I knew.

The next few weeks passed in anticipation of what was to

come.

On July 1, 1963, Kamala's sister Usha was married to Pandu Chintamani in a grand wedding ceremony. I was invited to the wedding as a guest by Kamala. I got an opportunity to meet all her family members then. After the wedding, the newly married couple went on a short honeymoon to Srinagar in Kashmir.

Soon, most unexpectedly, tragedy struck the family. Ramu, then only fifteen years old, passed away on July 5 from cerebral polio. Kamala's parents were devastated by the sudden loss. Usha and Pandu hurriedly returned from their honeymoon vacation to console the bereaved parents.

On July 15, college reopened. After the sudden tragedy, Kamala's parents were reluctant to send her to college. She stayed home for a few days. Following a lot of discussion within the family, it was decided that she should continue to attend classes again.

Those days were very difficult for me. I knew that Kamala and her parents were overcome with grief. She would not talk to me, and walked with a heavy heart. She would sit in the class, brooding, without her charming, captivating smile, to which I had become accustomed. Only time could soften her sorrow.

I knew I had to cheer her up and console her. After a few days, I accompanied her one afternoon and boarded the bus to Sujan Singh Park. We sat silently for a while. Then I slowly started talking. Although this was no time to bring up the subject of our marriage, I had to discuss it. There were only a few days remaining before the thirty-day notice period would be over.

She understood the gravity of the situation. She said that the tragedy had overwhelmed the family. She was under intense mental pressure—the need to console her grief-stricken mother, the burden of our common "secret," and the necessity to go ahead with a clandestine civil marriage within a few days. It was awfully difficult to deal with such conflicting emotions. My heart bled for her.

We had only two options: one was to go ahead with our earlier plans and get married; the other was to postpone it indefinitely.

Both courses of action were risky. This was no enviable situation. But we knew we had to decide one way or the other. Time was of the essence.

I recalled what Shakespeare had written: "The course of true love never runs smooth." The bard's words repeatedly echoed in my heart. I was torn between my love for Kamala, who needed time to heal her sorrow, and the "cold necessity" to get on with the "business of our marriage"—there is no other way to describe the predicament I was in.

"What ye sow, thou shall reap." The truth of this saying sank into my head, again and again.

Most of my adult life thus far had been filled with circumstances and events that forced me to make quick decisions affecting the future. Indeed, everyone's life is subject to the same rule, and there is no escaping from its relentless logic. Once again, I was confronted with the need to make a momentous decision. Should we go ahead with our secret plan to get married, regardless of the present tragic situation in which Kamala was engulfed? Or should we allow ourselves to succumb to the tyranny of circumstances— beyond our control—and shelve our marriage plan?

Several thoughts were flashing through my mind. Some of the books on the subject of personal growth I had read had taught me about the need to act on one's inner convictions. Life is a one-way street. Lost opportunities never come back. I did not want our life to end like a Greek tragedy.

Our future now hung in the balance. Any recommendation, or should I say, decision, I made would be acceptable to Kamala. I knew she would go along with it. It was, indeed, all up to me now to make a choice. I searched my soul deeply for an answer. And the answer came out loud and clear:

"Get Married NOW."

"Don't let this opportunity pass."

"Love will triumph in the end."

94

My doubts were resolved. I told Kamala to get ready for our marriage on the August 2, 1963.

Our plan was that Kamala would come prepared to attend classes on that day, just as if it were a normal day. I would meet her at the Sujan Singh Park bus stop. Then we would go together to the marriage court. After our marriage, she would go back home, just as she did after class every day.

I requested three of my trusted friends to come to witness our marriage, as was required by law.

There was nothing more to be done, but wait for August 2.

Anxiety and anticipation kept me awake at nights.

On August 2, I reached the Sujan Singh Park bus stop early in the morning and waited for Kamala. She arrived, walking with her charming gait, smiling, as was her usual style. I was relieved and happy to see her thus. We got into a taxi and proceeded to the marriage court in Delhi. We were both too much preoccupied by conflicting emotions to do much talking along the way.

My friends were waiting in the court for us. The judge arrived, and we were soon seated. There were a few other people in the room.

The judge called our names. We stood up.

The judge asked us to come before him to solemnize our marriage. He looked at the petition in front of him. Suddenly, he remarked:

"According to this petition, Kamala was not yet eighteen years old when she applied for permission to marry. Therefore, this petition is out of order."

I stared at the petition and then addressed the judge: "Sir, she is eighteen years old. Her date of birth is the sixth of July 1945".

The judge: "She was not eighteen years old on June 2, when she signed the paper. A minor person cannot sign the petition."

I said: "Sir, we are sorry for the oversight. This was unintentional. It was truly an honest mistake on our part. We are here now. Please allow us to get married today."

The judge: "What is the hurry? You can sign another petition today, and come back to the court in thirty days. Then you would have fulfilled the law."

I replied: "Sir, that would be impossible. I am going to the United States at the end of this month for higher studies. I have already booked my air ticket. My university is expecting me. If we do not get married today, we will not be able to get married at a later time. We do not have thirty days to wait. Please allow us to get married NOW. PLEASE."

The judge pondered for a long time. It was agony waiting for his decision. He looked at us. He relented.

For me, time stood still.

"All right. I will permit it."

I said simply: "Thank you, sir."

Soon, the marriage formalities were over. We signed on the dotted line.

Now, at last, Gopal and Kamala were pronounced man and wife, Mr. and Mrs. Dorai!

I invited my friends to go with us to a nearby tea shop. All I could offer them was some tea and sweets to celebrate. They saw how happy we were.

They congratulated us. I thanked them for their assistance, and bid farewell.

Afterward, we got into a taxi. We drove back to Kamala's house, and I left her in front of her doorsteps. We said goodbye to each other. I went home.

I told my brothers Ramakrishnan and Vaitha about our marriage. I explained to them the circumstances of our courtship and the decision to get married. Both my younger brothers were very understanding. I told them that I would inform our parents later.

Then I went to bed.

The irony of our situation soon dawned on me, when I saw Kamala in my class the next day. She was still one of my students. I was still the teacher. Though we had changed our status privately, our respective positions in the college had not changed one bit. Sometimes, our capacity to hide our real thoughts, feelings or emotions is truly amazing. Kamala and I exchanged meaningful glances. I could hardly wait for the classes to be over in order to go out with my new wife.

One thing had changed overnight: my attitude to the whole world. I no longer felt that I had to be clandestine in taking Kamala out with me. A strange, unexplained courage had entered my whole being.

There were only three weeks left for me to go to America. I wanted to spend as much time with my wife as possible. But how could this be possible? She was still an "unmarried maiden" as far as the world was concerned. And a man could not be seen in the company of a maiden unless he was related to her, as sanctioned by society.

After class, we walked together for a short distance. I did not want to waste any more time waiting for the usual bus ride. We headed to Lodhi Gardens in a taxi. At last I could hold Kamala's hands for a little while longer. She eagerly concurred that we should spend more time together, at least for the next couple of days. She promised to come up with some excuse for us to stay together. But only for a few days, she reminded me gently. More than that would be difficult.

Both of us were wracking our brains about how best to spend the few precious hours we had. The time for rendezvous would soon be over. What should we do?

The next day, after class, we headed to my apartment. The landlady saw us enter the house. I greeted her, as usual, and introduced Kamala, without acknowledging that she was my wife. It would have been very hard to explain how I obtained a wife in

97

such a short time. Actually, I did not bother about such trivialities any more.

My brother Vaitha was at home, lying in bed, sick with jaundice. I introduced Kamala, and he was delighted to see his new "Bhabiji."

We could only be together for a short while. Soon Kamala had to return to her parent's home. It would have been impossible to prolong our secretive meeting much longer. Her mother would be worried sick. It was hard to come up with new excuses explaining why she was late.

For the next couple of days, we spent our afternoons together. But the situation was becoming difficult to manage. We could not go on with this ad hoc rendezvous every day without raising very inconvenient questions from Kamala's family. We were wondering what to do and how best to deal with the situation. Then it occurred to me that it would be wise to inform Kamala's parents about our marriage, though it was a risky step to take. I reasoned that informing them now would be far preferable to keeping the marriage a secret for long. What if something untoward happened to me while I was abroad? Kamala would be left alone without anybody to support and comfort her. The burden of having to keep our marriage a secret for many years, I thought, may overwhelm Kamala. Even though it sounded absurd, some traditional marriage proposal might come up (for consideration by her parents) while I was abroad. Such a possibility might entangle my wife in a hopelessly messy situation. How would she deal with this eventuality? How could she confront her parents and reveal that she was already someone else's wife? The absurdity of the situation was staring at us. We discussed the pros and cons of informing her parents. It was agreed that we should tell them the truth before my departure to America.

When? How? Where?

We decided that I should ask for a meeting with her parents. Undoubtedly, the sooner this was done, the better. There was no use in waiting till the last minute. Kamala thought it would be best if I faced her parents alone, without her by my side.

Of course we could not visualize how the parents would react to the bombshell news. It was probable that in their sudden shock, anger and frustration, they may even disown her completely. We had no idea how upset and unhappy they might be. They had just suffered the irreparable loss of a son. We feared that we would be adding "insult to injury" through this new revelation. Kamala knew very well how short-tempered her father, CRG, was. She shuddered at the possibility of confronting him after revealing the truth. In case CRG was unwilling to accept the "fait accompli," we reasoned, she would need to find a place to stay in my absence. Prudence dictated that we make a contingency plan for such an eventuality.

Since I was going abroad, and had very limited funds to spare, I thought I could persuade my Uncle Ponnanna to come to our rescue. Perhaps he would agree to accommodate Kamala for a couple of months until I made arrangements for her to join me in USA. He was the only family member I knew who might be sympathetic to our cause. He had moved to Jabalpur (in Central India) a few months back.

With these plans more or less chalked out in our minds, the next thing to do was to seek a meeting with Kamala's parents. I called CRG on the phone the next day and sought an urgent appointment in their home. With much reluctance, he agreed to meet me the following day at 10 a.m.

On that day, Kamala left home to attend college as usual. But instead of going to college, she came directly to my home. And I steeled myself for the task ahead of me. This was going to test all my wits. The day of reckoning had come.

Torn between loyalty to her parents and devotion to her husband, Kamala was totally helpless. An avalanche of conflicting emotions engulfed her. Anxiety about the forthcoming meeting was clearly visible on her sweet face. I tried to comfort her as much as I could. After reassuring her again, I hastened to my assigned task.

When I rang the bell, CRG opened the door. He and his wife Saroja greeted me cordially, and offered a cup of tea. I settled comfortably on the seat. The conversation that ensued was smooth at first, and gradually became an ordeal as it unwound. Here is how it proceeded:

CRG: "Kamala told me you are going to the USA to do a Ph.D. Congratulations. When are you leaving?"

Gopal: "I am scheduled to leave on the twenty-fifth of August. I have booked my ticket on Air India."

CRG: "Can I help you in any way? Is there anything I can do? Nowadays the foreign exchange rules are very strict. India's foreign exchange reserves are very low. Did you get sufficient exchange?"

Gopal: "Not really. As you said, the country cannot afford to give me any extra foreign exchange. I am allowed only eight dollars, which is the amount allowed by the government of India for any student going abroad. I don't think I will have any problem, though. The university has offered to give me an initial loan as soon as I reach there. That will tide me over the first few weeks. Then I will be getting an assistantship. So I am all set."

CRG: "How is Kamala doing in class? I think last year she was busy with a lot of things in college. She didn't do as well academically as I had expected."

Gopal: "She is fine. I think she is reading all the assignments. She sometimes asks questions in class. The other day, she came to my desk for help with a problem. I think she will do reasonably well in Economics.

"But I came here to ask for something very personal. Please let me explain why I came to see you."

CRG: "Go ahead."

Gopal: "This is very difficult for me. I don't know how to begin. I will try my best to be brief. Let me explain. Please do not misunderstand me. I came to request for the hand of your daughter

100

in marriage. We love each other very much."

By now, Kamala's mother, who was standing nearby, withdrew to the door near the kitchen. I could see the anxiety and strain building on her face. She was visibly shaken. CRG's whole facial expression had changed. He was becoming very uncomfortable.

CRG: "How can this be? You are her professor. How can you expect to marry her? She is hardly eighteen. I am not planning to get her married for several years."

Gopal: "I know. It just happened, without any deliberate plan on our part. We started talking to each other. She is very beautiful and talented. I had opportunities to get to know her last year when she was president of the Fine Arts Society. I was the faculty advisor. I find a lot of potential in her. If I weren't going to America soon, I wouldn't have come here like this to request you. Since I am going away, I thought I should do this before I leave. I do not want to lose her. I am not sure when I will come back."

CRG: "This is absolutely shocking. Who are you? When did this affair begin? Where did you meet her?"

Gopal: "I am very sorry to give you this shock. I know how you feel. It is like stealing your daughter. But we love each other. I know she loves me. We had a few conversations about mutual interests. We decided that I should come and talk to you before I left the country. We know society does not look kindly on it. I belong to the Iyer community. I was born in Kerala. My parents belong to a respected family there. My father is a schoolteacher, and also owns some land. I have several brothers and sisters. I am the second son. I am twenty-seven years old. I grew up in a place called Vilayur and had my high school education there. Thereafter I studied in Hyderabad and moved to Delhi in 1956. I got my MA in economics from Delhi. I worked in the All India Radio for a few years, and then became a lecturer in SV College last year. I will be glad to furnish my parents' address, and provide any other information you want. I want your consent to marry Kamala. I love her very much."

101

Looking at him, I could surmise that various emotions were crossing CRG's mind. His wife was now standing beside the kitchen door, listening to the conversation, and slowly started sobbing. I could see the tears roll down her cheeks. I felt awful, seeing her suffer. The whole atmosphere was charged with indescribable emotions. The tension in the room was unbearable. I tried to stay calm. I continued:

"Sir, I know the situation is very difficult. I am aware that your son Ramu passed away last month. Kamala told me everything. I am very sorry. You must be going through a lot. I didn't know what else to do. I did not want to go abroad without informing you about my feelings for Kamala. That is why I sought this meeting. Please understand. I will do anything to win her hand."

CRG: "I was unprepared for this turn of events, as you can see. I think you know that my daughter Usha got married last month. And then my son Ramu died suddenly. We cannot think of Kamala's marriage now. It is out of the question."

There was a long pause.

Then he continued: "I have no plans at all for that right now."

This was getting difficult. After a few moments passed, I said:

Gopal: "Sir, I understand your predicament very well. I know the situation first hand. We wanted to apprise you of our mutual love, and seek your permission for the marriage. Since I am going away, I had to come and see you right away."

CRG: "My daughter is not ready for marriage now. I really don't know your background. How do I know you are right for her? I will have to refuse. I think I will leave it there."

Gopal: "Sir, you have put me in a very awkward situation. I came here with the best of intentions. I am a very honorable person. My parents are very good people. You can ascertain for yourself. Let me give you their address. Please write to them."

CRG: "I know. I do not doubt your sincerity. It is just that I am not prepared for this kind of talk just now. Perhaps you can leave

102

now. Let me see."

He got up.

This was no time for beating around the bush. We had clearly come to the end of the conversation, as far as he was concerned. I knew I had to be absolutely blunt. I continued:

Gopal: "Sir, I want to tell you something more. Please sit down. Please prepare yourself for a shock."

CRG: "Yes? What is it?"

Gopal: "Sir, I must tell you something. Kamala and I are already married."

CRG: Visibly shaken—"My God! What? When? How?"

Gopal: "Kamala and I discussed this at great length. We knew you would not allow us to get married now because of the circumstances. I am going away to America. I may or may not be able to return within three years. We did not want to lose each other. We were afraid that if we did not get married right away, we might lose each other. The only way to deal with this was to get married first, and then inform our parents. So we had to rush into a registered marriage."

CRG: "When did this happen?"

Gopal: "Last week, actually, on August second. At first we thought we should keep quiet about it, until I returned after my studies. Then we decided we should inform you now, without waiting. We thought that this was the right thing to do. That is why I am here. Please understand. Please pardon me. I know how you feel. I am really sorry that I caused you all this anxiety."

By now, it appeared that CRG had partially recovered from his shock. He had some time to collect himself. The pain and anger were clearly visible on his face.

We sat there in silence for a while. At last, he said:

CRG: "All right. I see what you have done. What is your plan now?"

Gopal: "My plan was to come and tell you the truth. I wanted you to know what we have done. I have not yet informed my parents. I am writing to them. I will be leaving on August twenty-fifth. I have only a few days left."

CRG: "Then please postpone your trip. Let me see what to do. Perhaps I want to talk to some of my friends and decide the next step. In any case, you must postpone your trip."

Gopal: "Yes, sir. I will do what you say. But the university asked me to come at the end of August. I can wait a few more days."

CRG: "Good. Please do that. Let us see what we should do. Call me tomorrow. Then we can talk some more."

Gopal: "Thank you, sir. I will do what you say. I will call you tomorrow morning. Goodbye."

I got up. I bowed before him. I left with my dignity and also my senses in complete control. This was an ordeal that tested my diplomatic skills to the limit. I thought I handled the situation as best as I was capable of. I had accomplished what I came for.

Kamala was waiting for me anxiously in my place. I related to her what happened. We proceeded to her home. I knew she was going to face the toughest interrogation of her life. I hoped she would handle it well. I kissed her goodbye, until the next day.

# Chapter 12

## A Traditional Wedding Ceremony

This chapter is short and sweet.

When I went back to CRG's home the following day, one of his friends, Mr. Vasu, was present. CRG told me that Mr.Vasu had come to help them sort out the appropriate steps to be taken to deal with our "marriage situation." The family needed the assistance of a trusted adviser, an objective voice, to handle the "problem." Mr.Vasu and CRG asked me many questions about my past life, as well as about our courtship and marriage. We talked for about two hours. They seemed satisfied with all the answers I provided. Relieved to find out Kamala was in good hands, they told me that they would consult with a priest to fix a date for a "proper wedding" at an early date. It would be a simple Hindu religious ceremony. A few of the family's relatives and friends would be invited to attend the function. I was told that such a "proper wedding ceremony" was required to sanctify our civil marriage, and to signify that the family had accepted me as a suitable son-in-law.

After some more discussion, CRG asked me if I wanted to invite anyone from my side for the wedding. I replied that I had two younger brothers with me, and a few other friends whom I would like to invite. It was unlikely that my parents could travel to Delhi at such short notice.

The meeting had gone very well, and I was relieved that our decision to inform Kamala's parents about our secret matrimony turned out to be right. Indeed, I was happy that they wanted to conduct a "proper wedding ceremony." At last Kamala and I could stay together and be accepted as a legitimate married couple by our families as well as society.

The wedding ceremony took place on September 9, 1963, at CRG's house. It was a simple, dignified event. About forty guests were present. Kamala and I were overjoyed when we garlanded each other in front of the assembled guests. As per the ancient Vedic Hindu marriage rites, we took seven steps around the Sacred Fire—Saptapati—signifying our lifelong promise to:

Live in friendship and harmony

Love, honor and cherish each other

Provide sustenance and support for each other

Bring forth progeny and educate them to be good citizens

Make charitable contributions to worthy causes

Serve society and discharge our social obligations

Strengthen our married bonds throughout life

These prescriptions for an enduring and successful marriage were given by ancient Indian sages and seers millenniums ago. We understood their significance. We respectfully accepted them as guiding principles for our future life together.

During the wedding ceremony, I was especially happy to observe that Kamala's mother, Saroja, had accepted me as her son-in-law. Although I had snatched away her daughter without her prior approval or knowledge, she seemed to have forgiven me. Despite the mental agony and anguish she had suffered, this auspicious event seemed to have restored a semblance of calmness and peace to mind to her. Being accepted as a legitimate member of their family was important to me. I felt grateful for her kindness. Her blessing of our marriage gave it permanence and legitimacy.

I spent the next three days with my wife in the home of my new parents-in-law. It was a memorable and sweet honeymoon. Those were among the happiest days of our life. Kamala was radiant with joy. I felt very proud to be her husband, and being accepted as a member of the family.

# PART II: AMERICA

## Chapter 13

## Arrival in the United States

Preparations were now in full swing for my impending departure to the United States. I had booked my flight to New York by Air India for September 12, 1963. There was not a whole lot to pack. All my personal belongings could be put into a small suitcase I had borrowed from a dear friend. Indian foreign exchange regulations allowed me only eight dollars to take with me.

I bid a fond farewell to my brothers, friends and new relatives. Leaving Kamala behind was not easy. Until I could secure a visa for her, she would have to stay back. I hoped that she would be able to join me within a couple of months.

Transcontinental flights in 1963 took almost twice as much time as they did forty years later. My plane was a small 707 Boeing, carrying approximately eighty passengers. This was my maiden flight. After stopping at several airports along the way for hours at a time, the flight finally landed in New York. Suddenly I found myself in an alien world, with strange people speaking the English (American) language with a totally different accent. Sometimes it took me a while to understand what was being said.

After completing the immigration formalities, I boarded a connecting flight to Detroit, which reached there around 9 p.m. At the airport, a stranger appeared before me and introduced himself as Mr. Alexander, sent by the Foreign Student Office of Wayne State University. Soon, my host and I were on our way inside a spacious car, speeding our way to his home in nearby Dearborn. The kind reception I received, as well as the sights and sounds I was experiencing, made a great impression on me. The brilliant night sky, lit by the headlights of the speeding automobiles on the Ford Expressway, was a great contrast to the dimly lit streets of Delhi. To my surprise, despite the large number of cars on the road, the traffic was flowing smoothly. This was truly amazing, compared to the chaotic, zigzag and unruly pattern of Delhi's streets. Soon, we were in Mr. Alexander's house.

Mrs. Alexander welcomed me as soon as we got out of the car. She was a charming hostess. Her warm and gracious hospitality was notable. It seemed as if I had known her all my life. The conversation flowed smoothly, and I felt quite at home. My previous apprehensions about how I would feel after landing on American soil seemed groundless. I was happy and relieved. Since I was very tired from the long journey, my hosts urged me to retire to bed after an hour or so. Soon I was asleep in a large bed in a very large room. I had never experienced this kind of luxury before!

The following morning, Mr. Alexander drove me to the YMCA lodge near the university campus in Detroit, where they had arranged a room for me. I was scheduled to report to the Economics Department around noon.

With a map in hand, I found my way to Cass Avenue, and walked past the Old Main Building to Mackenzie Hall. I took an elevator to the eighth floor, and was soon in front of the reception desk of the Economics Department. I had reached my destination.

Soon I was ushered into the office of Dr. Mark Kahn, Chairman of the Economics Department. I spent about half an hour talking with him. Thereafter, I filled out all the papers he handed over to me to complete the admission formalities. I was also given an envelope containing one hundred dollars. This was a temporary loan to tide me over until the first paycheck, which would be distributed in two weeks.

Afterward, I went to the Foreign Student Office, located on the fifth floor of Mackenzie Hall. Mrs. Boltwood, the Foreign Student Adviser, greeted me with her smiling demeanor and a welcoming handshake. Her office was totally dedicated to helping all the incoming foreign students in every possible way. The office staff was extremely courteous, and they answered my numerous questions patiently. I felt very welcome and wanted. Their welcoming attitude and willingness to help certainly eased the adjustment problem of newly arrived foreigners like me.

Mrs. Boltwood informed me that I would have to wait a few weeks to complete the processing of Kamala's visa application. A foreign student could bring his spouse to America only on the condition that the latter was not allowed to work. At first, I was told that my assistantship income of $1,900 was insufficient for a married couple to live in Detroit. I told Mrs. Boltwood that we got married less than a week ago, and that my wife's presence was imperative for my physical and mental wellbeing. I also told her that with my expected additional summer stipend of about $400 we would be able to manage our finances, though frugally. She promised to give me all possible assistance.

The next task was to find a suitable abode. The FSO gave me a few addresses where I could make inquiries about cheap, temporary housing for students.

Within a couple of days, I visited the Student Housing Office and put in a request for an apartment. The accommodations would be available in a month or two.

Wandering the streets in the vicinity of university campus, I walked into a doughnut shop. Fresh doughnuts were being cooked in a big frying pan. In my innocence (should I say "ignorance") I thought the doughnuts were like our South Indian "vadai," a delicious salty snack (made from lentils) I was fond of. When I put the doughnut into my mouth, I was totally surprised to find that it tasted sweet. Its taste and texture intrigued me. Similarly, I also visited a pizza shop, and again mistook the thick, flat and rounded pizza pie for an "adai," which I used to eat in India. A staple of the typical South Indian vegetarian diet, adai is made from various lentils and rice—grounded together—and cooked on top of a stove.

To my surprise, the pizza was unlike any adai I had ever eaten! This reminded me of the saying that "appearances are deceptive." Though I did not much like the doughnut, I found the taste of the pizza to my liking.

109

In a few days, I plunged into the academic life and routine. There were many courses I had to take to complete the curriculum. The whole course work would take about two years, I estimated. During the first semester, I enrolled in just a couple of classes: Prof. Seltzer's seminar entitled "Monetary and Fiscal Policy," and a mathematics course. These turned out to require much more study than I had imagined. The seminar involved a very long reading list of books, journal articles and other research material. In my earlier college education, I had not encountered so much reading for any single course. It needed a lot of getting used to. I found the seminar extremely interesting and learned a great deal about the federal reserve system, its purposes and functions, American financial institutions, capital markets and implementation of monetary policy. The course provided excellent grounding for future courses and studies.

I used to visit the Foreign Student Office almost every alternate day to seek information of one kind or another. During one such visit, I learned about the Indian Students' Association on campus. Mrs. Boltwood introduced me to its office bearers. I soon found out that Wayne State University had a fairly large body of Indian students, numbering about 110 at that time. This was indeed welcome news. I got to know some of the married Indian students. A couple of them invited me to their homes. It was a pleasure to meet those families and to taste some Indian food, which I was sorely missing for a while. The families made me feel at home, and even allowed me to play a musical tape that I had brought along for listening.

The following days and weeks passed very fast. The F2 visa for Kamala was at last obtained. I also managed to get a small two-bedroom apartment, leased by the university's housing office, for married graduate student families. It was situated about two miles away from campus, in the tall Jeffries Building near the John Lodge Expressway. I was overjoyed that Kamala would soon be able to join me.

She arrived early in November 1963. Mrs. Boltwood accompanied me to the Detroit airport to fetch her. When we saw Kamala

110

emerge from the crowd of arriving passengers, Mrs. Boltwood commented on her youth and beauty. Kamala was wearing a colorful sari. Though tired from the long journey, Kamala was beaming at us. We drove to our apartment. I thanked Mrs. Boltwood for her help in securing the visa so soon.

Within a few days, we settled down to our new lifestyle. Mrs. Boltwood, mindful of our need for different household items, had arranged to obtain a few essential cooking vessels, pots and pans from her network of donors. One of her friends invited us to give a talk in their local church. We were happy to do so. We talked about our respective socio-economic backgrounds, schooling and life in India. During the talk, the audience learned about our recent marriage as well as the fact that we were just setting up our household in Detroit for the first time.

To our complete surprise and utter delight, the next day we found several members of the church bringing all sorts of furniture and utensils to our apartment. We marveled at their generosity and thoughtfulness in providing these household essentials without any request on our part. This was indeed a remarkable welcome gesture. Most of the things we needed for the household were now in place. With our meager financial resources, it would not have been possible to purchase all these items, at least for a while. We felt very grateful for the unexpected help we got.

Kamala became a frequent guest speaker at many churches, local schools and other civil organizations. She enjoyed these speaking invitations. It kept her busy and usefully occupied, besides providing opportunities to get to know the communities around us. Such meetings were also widely reported in the local *Detroit Press*, and she got some unexpected publicity.

The Jeffries Housing Project consisted of two tall, fourteen-storied buildings with a couple of hundred apartment units between them. Wayne State University had earmarked about fifty of these units for married student families. The rent was nominal. We paid only seventy dollars in monthly rent, which was about a third of our income. As we did not own a car, we used to carry grocery bags home from the nearby supermarket in our hands.

Soon we got to know some of our student family neighbors. Among them were a dozen foreign students, including some Indians. Most of these foreign student wives had much in common. (Almost all the foreign graduate students happened to be men.) When their spouses were away at school with their academic work, the ladies used to get together and help each other in various ways. Our neighbors, the McDonalds and the Munns, were always there to lend us a helping hand whenever we needed. Kamala developed good rapport with her new friends. Two of these, Vimal Marwah and her husband Jawahar, from Gwalior (India), became very close to us. Graduate studies involved spending a lot of time in the university library, even on weekends. The men were always away at school. The resulting loneliness experienced by the students' wives was somewhat mitigated by the mutual support and constant company they provided each other.

One particular incident stands out in my memory. One day, sometime during the first semester of my studies, I had to stay back in school to complete a writing assignment. I had no idea that I would be very late in going home. Usually I would go home by 6 p.m. On that day, I could not be home before 9 p.m. I could not communicate with Kamala about the long delay either. When I returned home, I found that the door was locked. Kamala was nowhere to be seen. I panicked. Then I knocked on the door of my neighbors, the McDonalds, to make inquiries. I found Kamala sitting there, sobbing all the while. She had gone to Mrs. McDonald seeking comfort and solace, not knowing what to make of my unusual absence. The neighbor was trying to console her as much as possible. I was admonished profusely for my wanton neglect of my loving wife! Kamala was furious with me for a long time. I learned my lesson—that I should call and inform my wife about any possible delay in coming home in the future.

The first winter in Detroit was a novel experience for us. We had never seen snowfall before. One day in early November I felt large flakes of some white stuff hitting my face. At first it looked like a locust swarm to me. I soon realized that the "locusts" were quite cold! And they started sticking to the ground too. Soon the ground was covered with them. I realized immediately that winter was around the corner. The cold wind was hitting my face rather fiercely. A sudden chill entered my whole body, and I ran home as fast as I could. Very soon, the whole ground was covered with thick, white snow.

As we were not prepared for Detroit's celebrated cold weather, we did not have heavy winter clothing. Soon I found myself shopping for a woolen overcoat in a nearby Goodwill Thrift store. Apart from a used black and white TV set that we purchased around this time, the winter coat was the only major item of expenditure in our tight budget. The income I earned as a teaching assistant was adequate for our basic needs, nothing beyond that. In fact, we used to save a small amount of surplus money every now and then.

Although we had heard about many of the American holidays when we were in India, we were not at all familiar with Thanksgiving. When the big Thursday in November arrived, we were invited to have dinner with a host family. Early in the afternoon, our hosts from Dearborn came to pick us up. They were cooking all afternoon for the big feast. I was curious to find out how the custom of having a big turkey for Thanksgiving dinner came about. We soon learned about the Pilgrims who landed at Plymouth Rock in Massachusetts, their meeting with the local Indian tribes, and the dinner they had together on that cold winter day in 1621. Being a vegetarian, Kamala felt very sorry for all those turkeys being slaughtered throughout America for that day's big dinner! Such was her innocence that she actually sat and prayed for the birds!

The first Christmas season for us in America soon arrived. Mrs. Boltwood had a list of host families who wanted to entertain foreign students. Mr. and Mrs. Wilmoth of Farmington, Michigan, invited us to spend our Christmas holidays with them. Both of them were teachers in a local high school. They had two children, Noel and Penny, about twelve and ten years of age. We delighted in their company. The spirit of the holiday season and its associated trappings, such as the Christmas tree, beautiful lighting of the

113

neighborhood homes, family visits, festivities, elaborate dinners and gift giving, all these traditions were quite novel for us. The Wilmoth family soon became our lifelong friends, and we have maintained our close friendship with them ever since.

The first winter season in Detroit was memorable. The biting cold was at first difficult to get used to. Walking on the slippery road was always hazardous. I had been wearing a pair of shoes brought from India, which were definitely not suitable for walking on snow and ice. I also did not have sufficient warm clothing other than the second-hand jacket I had bought recently. I had to walk the two-mile distance from home to school almost every day, sometimes through knee-deep snow. Snow had piled high on all the sidewalks, and I found it hard to negotiate my way through those snow banks. One day, the Wilmoths took us for a drive over the frozen lake surface. There were a few people digging deep holes in the middle of the lake, through the thick, frozen ice, looking for fish. I was told that this was a great sport. I could not believe that such a large body of water could freeze like this. The temperature sometimes hit below negative twenty degrees Farenheit. The weather was bitterly cold during those four winter months. It was extremely difficult for us to get used to the first winter in Detroit.

Our earlier apprehensions about our ability to adapt to our new environment were unwarranted. The new friendships we developed, as well as the constant willingness of our neighbors to render help, eased the process considerably. Perhaps the major difficulty we faced was in securing the spices and condiments needed for cooking our Indian vegetarian food. The only place where we could buy these items was a Middle Eastern store, Kalustyans, in Manhattan, New York. So these items were occasionally mail-ordered from there. Many of the vegetables and fruits (which we needed) were not readily available in the corner grocery stores. But they were frequently available in the outdoor Eastern Market in downtown Detroit on weekends. We depended on our friends, the Marwahs, for transportation to take us there. Thus, our adjustment to life in America proceeded smoothly.

114

Early in 1965, we found out that Kamala was pregnant. In September, her friends got together and held a baby shower for her. This too was a novel experience for Kamala. We were delighted that several of the clothing and other items needed for the new baby were being assembled long before the baby arrived.

One day, Kamala expressed a desire to go out for dinner. In those days we were not used to having dinner in a restaurant. There were hardly any places serving purely vegetarian food. So we walked on Woodward Avenue, Detroit's long commercial artery, in search of a place to eat. We walked a long distance, and finally decided to have a pizza, as we did not find any other suitable place to eat. After dinner, we started walking back home. Kamala was exhausted. It still didn't occur to me to hire a taxi. As she was walking with sandals on her feet, which were not suitable for such long walks, she was experiencing a lot of pain. She was also in an advanced state of pregnancy. The weather was getting quite cold. I write about this now because she has often pointed out this episode as evidence of my "lack of sensitivity." I realized then that I should not have allowed her to walk under those difficult circumstances. Life is full of opportunities to learn from one's mistakes.

Our first baby, Tara, was born on October 19, 1965. Our good friends, Vimal and Jawahar, drove us to Detroit Women's Hospital late at night for the delivery. Kamala had a very long and difficult labor. I walked up and down, for a very long time, outside the delivery room. There was not much else I could do, except wait and pray.

We did not have much guidance in bringing up our new baby, other than Dr. Spock's *Baby and Child Care*. We got whatever little help we needed from our friends. Tara grew up fast. When she was born, she was a tiny baby, weighing only about six and a half pounds.

Tara's first birthday is etched in our minds forever. We wanted to have a big birthday party for her. We had invited about thirty guests, consisting of most of the American and foreign families we knew. All day was spent cooking and preparing various Indian delicacies with the assistance of our close Indian friends. We had nicely decorated the basement of the building for the big party with colorful birthday balloons and ribbons. The birthday cake had a picture of Tara's beautiful face in the center of it. I don't know how the bakery did this without a digital camera!

As the evening drew to a close, Kamala started getting uneasy. Gradually, she started to feel quite sick. Despite this, we wanted to continue with the party. In a little while, Vimal took charge of the arrangements and assured us that she would handle everything smoothly. Before most of the guests had assembled, we decided that it would be prudent to go to the hospital. We rushed to the emergency room at the nearby Henry Ford Hospital. There we found out that Kamala had a miscarriage. She was advised to rest and recoup. Actually, we did not know beforehand that she was pregnant, and the insensitive doctor asked her if she had planned this miscarriage deliberately!

We returned in a few hours and attended the first birthday party for Tara. Kamala sat in a corner to rest; meanwhile, our good friend Vimal had taken care of the guests. The birthday party went on smoothly, with Tara running around to the delight of everyone present.

Tara grew up very fast. I used to take her out almost every day, often carrying her on my shoulders. One day I took Tara with me to get some bread and milk from the corner store. I found it diffi-cult to carry her and the grocery bag at the same time. There was a cart lying around, and I put Tara and the groceries in the cart and pushed it for a while. There was a long pathway with a gentle slope in front of our apartment building. When I was a distance away from the entrance of the building, I let go of the cart with the baby placed on top of it! The cart suddenly took off, speeding its way down the pathway. I panicked. I ran fast to get hold of the cart, but it seemed to run away from me even faster. Before I had time to catch it, the cart hit the big entrance door to the building and rolled over. Tara fell to the ground, bleeding profusely. Her upper lip had been sliced by the impact. We rushed her to the hospital, and sev-eral stitches had to be put on her upper lip. The wound healed

116

within a few days, but the scar resulting from the accident is still visible on Tara. The incident taught me to be very careful with children and to be extra cautious when they are being pushed in a baby carriage. It was an emotionally expensive lesson for me.

# Chapter 14

## Graduate Student

My main mission in coming to America was to study for the Ph.D. degree in Economics. After our home life was set on a firm footing, I could devote myself to my studies without too many distractions. And this I did zealously. All the required and elective courses I needed to take followed in smooth succession. Within two years, I was ready to take the preliminary qualifying examination. This was followed by the "oral" examination.

I used to go to school almost every day, even when classes were not scheduled. The environment at school was conducive to academic work. Some of the Ph.D. students used to get together on weekends, discussing various topics and problems covered in our courses. We used to gather together in a corner library room and work out the problems on the board. This library room was my favorite study center. Adjacent to Mackenzie Hall was the Detroit Public Library building. Within a few months, I became a frequent visitor there. I persuaded the library staff to provide me with a small carrel, in which I collected all the books and journals required for my reading. The DPL was a very quiet place, and I could escape there without being disturbed by anyone.

Apart from a small number of required courses, the majority of the courses I took were electives. There was a great deal of freedom to choose one's elective courses. My favorite electives were International Economics and Human Capital. I really enjoyed reading and learning numerous theories and empirical studies dealing with topics in these areas.

The academic environment at WSU was very conducive to studies. Everyone I knew seemed to be highly motivated. How much you studied, and how well, were pretty much up to you. Nobody was pushing you to do anything. The professors expected you to do all the reading assignments. It was up to the individual students to pursue whatever goals they had set for themselves. I found most of the graduate students (such as myself) seriously pursuing their cherished goals. They appeared to be a highly motivated bunch. I knew that my own future depended on how well I did in my academic work.

After completing the qualifying "prelims" and the orals, it was time to prepare a proposal for the dissertation. I spent a couple of months researching and studying potential topics. The interrelationship between international trade and economic growth fascinated me. In my earlier course work, I had made a presentation on "Trade as an Engine of Economic Growth." This was a hot topic in the 1960s. There was considerable discussion going on in the academic journals about whether free trade helped or hampered the economic development of "emerging nations."

At the same time, another topic that caught my attention was the phenomenon of foreign students coming to the United States to seek advanced degrees. There were several thousand foreign graduate students and many more undergraduate students who were studying in America. A large percentage of these students returned to their homelands upon graduation. However, a significant number opted to stay here to get further practical training. A good number of them extended their stay indefinitely, becoming "de facto" migrants, or non-returnees. This state of affairs had become a topic of considerable discussion among economists and policy makers because of its varied economic/social impact on the countries of origin (as well as the United States).

I found this topic very interesting. Therefore, I decided to pursue it in more depth. Accordingly, I prepared a dissertation proposal on the topic of "Economics of the International Flow of Students: A Cost-Benefit Analysis." This proposal was submitted to the dissertation committee for approval.

After making appropriate modifications to the thesis proposal as per the advice of my professors, I submitted it to the Ford Foundation for funding. The Ford Foundation had solicited dissertation proposals from graduate economics departments throughout the

United States. My topic was approved and chosen for funding. I was awarded a two-year Ford Foundation Dissertation Fellowship. This freed me from the necessity of teaching (assistantship) on the WSU campus for the duration of the fellowship.

As soon as they completed the qualifying and oral examinations, various colleges/universities usually offered full-fledged teaching jobs to Ph.D. candidates. Usually, such teaching positions were called "instructorships." Many a time, job offers in the rank of assistant professors were also common. Such full-time teaching jobs paid four or five times the salary typically earned by graduate teaching assistants who were writing Ph.D. dissertations. The economic pressure to take up these teaching jobs (rather than continue as graduate teaching assistants) was great because of the big salary differentials.

I found myself in such a situation. When I became eligible, I had appeared for an interview for a teaching position at Albion College in Michigan. Several weeks following the interview, I was offered an assistant professorship there on an initial starting salary of $9,000. I found this salary offer irresistible, and had decided to accept it.

Around this time, the Ford Foundation Dissertation Fellowship came through. It would provide an annual stipend of $3,600 for two years. The higher salary and position offered by Albion College was tempting for an income-starved candidate such as myself.

Dr. Mark Kahn, Chairman of the Economics Department, understood my predicament. He called me into his office to discuss the matter. He convinced me that accepting the Albion offer would compromise my chances of completing my Ph.D. dissertation. He cited previous cases of several candidates who had accepted similar teaching jobs and then failed to complete their dissertation for several years. The teaching schedule, committee assignments and other academic responsibilities of college teaching would interfere with the concentrated work needed to complete a dissertation.

Dr. Kahn strongly advised me to turn down the Albion job offer and concentrate on my dissertation work.

121

I concurred readily with his advice. Without hesitation, I embarked on my research on a full-time basis. Later experience taught me that Dr. Kahn's advice was absolutely correct. I was very glad he steered me in the right direction before I succumbed to the temptations of the Almighty Dollar.

From September 1965 until the summer of 1967 I was fully absorbed in my studies and research. There was a lot of work to be done. Some of the data I needed for the empirical portion of my dissertation was not readily available from published sources. I spent a lot of time corresponding with various research institutions, government agencies and private sources to gather the required data. With the able guidance and timely assistance of my dissertation advisors, I made good, steady progress. The first draft of the Ph.D. thesis was under preparation by the summer of 1967. A few of the chapters had been completed.

Then suddenly, urban riots broke out in Detroit, Newark and Los Angeles. Racial tensions were high. We found ourselves right in the midst of the worst arson and looting Detroit had witnessed. There were several gunfights and fires in the buildings near our Jeffries neighborhood. Unfortunately, a Turkish graduate student was gunned down while walking to his home. People were running away with stolen goods everywhere around us. We were scared that our own building would be attacked. It was full of foreign student families. Some of the local American students packed up and left for their parental homes seeking safety. We decided to run for safety ourselves.

Our friends, Rohini and Girish Shah, who had a car, were getting ready to go to Ann Arbor. They were going to stay with a friend there. They asked us to join them. We grabbed Tara along with some needed baby clothing and started to go downstairs from the fifth floor, where our apartment was located. Suddenly I remembered that the few chapters of my dissertation draft were left in my school briefcase. This was a most precious item, and I could not, and certainly would not, want to leave it behind. So I took my dissertation draft along with me. It was the fruit of my labors during the previous year.

After two or three days of violence and much destruction, the urban riots were over. We returned to Detroit. Although some of the apartments had been looted and sacked, our place was untouched.

After returning from Ann Arbor, I redoubled my efforts to give finishing touches to my dissertation. Within a month, I was able to do so. I submitted the draft to my advisors and awaited their verdict. At last, I had accomplished a major task. Now it was time to relax a little, and attend to other matters.

# Chapter 15

## A Long Road Trip In Search of a Career

Anticipating the completion of my thesis in 1967, I had been looking for an academic job. It was customary for the university to help Ph.D. candidates in their job quests. The Economics Department was assisting me to secure a suitable employment contract. With their assistance, I got an interview with Wheaton College in Norton, Massachusetts, for an assistant professorship. Soon after the interview, I was offered employment, and was asked to join Wheaton in September 1967.

Now I needed to learn driving to get around town. Until now, we were solely dependent on the goodwill of our friends to take us out and around during emergencies. It was high time to become self-sufficient in our need for mobility. This matter could not be postponed any longer. So I enrolled in a driving class. I took six hours of driving lessons. This was indeed a challenging task for me. With much trepidation, I was soon by myself, alone in a car, negotiating traffic on the streets in my neighborhood. I knew I had to do it; there was no other way. One of the scariest experiences of my life was the day when I found myself on the John C. Lodge Expressway in Detroit. Joining the speedy traffic going over sixty-five miles per hour made me nervous and sweaty, to say the least. I somehow survived the ordeal, and came home safe. I was proud of my accomplishment that day. It was no mean task, considering my unfamiliarity in dealing with traffic until then, at the ripe old age of thirty-two. I remembered the instructions of my driving instructor—how to merge with speedy traffic from the ramp; how to change lanes; how to give turn signals; how to adjust the mirrors; how to follow and adjust to traffic conditions; and how to exit from the expressway. (I could then relate my own new driving experience to that of a senior citizen student who was happy to attend college for the first time in her life, along with much younger classmates.)

With the assistance of my friend Jawahar, who worked for the Ford Motor Company, I purchased a new Ford automobile during the summer of 1967. It was financed with a loan from the Detroit Teachers Credit Union. The cost of the car was about $2,700. Along with our friends, we took a trip in my new car to Mackinac Island in Northern Michigan for a leisurely vacation.

At last, we were ready to leave Detroit, as my Ph.D. thesis was almost complete. Those four years spent in the Motor City were memorable. We cherish it dearly to this day. We packed our few belongings, loaded our car, and headed toward Massachusetts.

I was now ready and eager to move to the next stage of our life. On our way to Norton, we decided to travel through Canada and visit the 1967 World Expo in Montreal. We stayed there for almost a week. A new chapter in our life would soon begin.

Along the way, we had a couple of small misadventures. When we reached Montreal, it was late at night. We were tired and hungry after a very long drive. We had been driving since morning, almost continuously for ten hours. In our desire to have a quick dinner, we entered the first restaurant we saw, which happened to be serving elegant French cuisine. (Montreal is the second largest French-speaking city after Paris; it is famous for its Parisian culture and cuisine.) After we sat there for a while, the waitress appeared with the menu. We were not familiar with French food (most of which happened to be non-vegetarian). Since we were vegetarians, we realized that it was a mistake to have gone into a French restaurant for dinner. I apologized profusely for this misstep, asked to be excused, and got out of that establishment in a hurry. After some exploration, we found a small eating place where we had a hearty cheese sandwich and milk. Reflecting on my experience, I was reminded of the old saying, "Look before you leap." Henceforth, I decided to investigate carefully what type of food was being served in any restaurant before sitting down for dinner. (Nowadays, it is easier to do this, because many eating establishments in big cities post their menu in front of their entrance doors.)

Continuing our journey toward Norton, we reached downtown Boston late in the afternoon. There, we got caught in a big rush-hour traffic jam. I had no idea how long we were going to be stuck on the crowded highway ahead of me. It seemed prudent to take the first available exit and look for an alternate, less-crowded route. I took a detour, which happened to lead directly into the Callahan Tunnel, headed in the direction of Logan Airport. This was getting completely away from where I wanted to go. Having entered the tunnel, I could not turn around and head back! After going through the long tunnel, I paid the mandatory toll and quickly turned around in the opposite direction. After a while, I ended up on some side road without any idea where I was headed. Having only limited experience of driving through crowded traffic in a big metropolis, I again made a wrong turn, and entered the Callahan Tunnel a second time! It was the last place I wanted to be; but there was nothing I could do but proceed. Imagine my consternation and frustration at my own stupidity!

That "there is bound to be light at the end of the tunnel" was the only consolation now. I took several deep breaths and proceeded for the tunnel exit. Finally, when I reached the end of the tunnel, the tollbooth attendant recognized me and kindly inquired what was going on. I related my unhappy experience. The angel took pity on me and offered to waive the toll this time around. He gave me clear directions about how to find the road leading to my desired destination. I thanked him profusely and was finally headed in the right direction.

My impatience and hurry had cost me an hour's extra delay, in addition to a nerve-racking driving record. I resolved that I would henceforth study road maps more carefully and learn to take in stride unavoidable traffic jams and unexpected roadside delays while driving. These are the inevitable hazards of modern travel. Everyone needs to put up with them, however unpleasant the ordeal. Otherwise they result in greater stress and raise our blood pressure, not to speak of lightening our wallets. Mistakes and misadventures often teach us valuable lessons.

I had single-handedly driven several hundred miles that day. At that time, Kamala had not learned to drive. Eventually, we reached Norton around 10 p.m. The owners of the little house that we had rented, Mr. and Mrs. Arena, welcomed us warmly. Knowing that we had a toddler with us, they had filled the refrigerator with staples such as milk, eggs, bread and cheese. Their thoughtfulness and hospitality were definitely heartwarming. Such little acts of kindness go a long way in making life a little more pleasant; they often help to smooth out the rough edges of life. It certainly eased my strained back and taut nerves that day.

# Chapter 16

## Triumphs and Setbacks

Norton is a small, rural town in southeastern Massachusetts, situated between Boston and Providence, Rhode Island. The beautiful campus of Wheaton College, a small liberal arts college, is located there. We had temporarily rented a small house within a short distance from the college campus. In contrast to the hustle and bustle of metropolitan Detroit, Norton was a typical, picturesque New England town. It remained very rural, much as it had for most of its history. In a few days, we settled down in our new surroundings.

My teaching job at Wheaton College was very enjoyable. Most of the classes were small in size, probably with no more than ten students. The students were generally very intelligent and motivated to learn. Many of them came from neighboring states, and some from a dozen or so foreign countries. The total size of the student body was about 1,300 and the faculty size was about 140. The academic environment was very conducive to teaching and learning.

In addition to its excellent academic programs, Wheaton also had modern extracurricular facilities. It had many state-of-the-art facilities for sports and recreation. I started playing tennis there for the first time. Although rather clumsy and awkward at first, I soon picked up the game with the assistance of a tennis veteran, Nancy Norton, who patiently coached me in the nuances of the game. In addition to several fine tennis courts, there was a good gym center with badminton courts, where Kamala and I often played with other faculty members.

The campus contained a good library, arts center and fine music/recording facilities. There also was a kindergarten for children of the faculty. Norton was an ideal place to bring up a young family. Tara enjoyed running around the sprawling grounds of the college campus. We made friends with lots of faculty members, and often invited each other for dinner.

At the end of the first semester, in December 1967, we went back to Detroit to participate in the graduation ceremonies at Wayne State University. This was the occasion when the Ph.D. degree was awarded to me. Our friends, Carol and Frank Kot, with whom we stayed as guests, accompanied us to the convocation ceremonies. Their genuine love and enthusiasm for my academic achievements made me realize, once again, how fortunate I was to have such good and caring friends. Without their full encouragement and constant help, I could not have accomplished what I did. It is indeed a pleasure and a pleasant duty to acknowledge how much they contributed to our mental and psychic wellbeing during our stay in Detroit.

At Wheaton College, I had the opportunity to host Mr. Jon Higgins, a notable, American musicologist and teacher of South Indian (or Carnatic) music, who taught at Wesleyan University. It was a joy to watch Mr. Higgins sing intricate and melodious ragas to an enthralled audience of students, faculty and music lovers, who had probably never heard this kind of music previously.

During 1968, I obtained a General Electric Summer Fellowship to attend a month-long seminar at the University of Virginia in Charlottesville. We drove down there, and on our way we saw many worthwhile tourist attractions. We especially enjoyed visiting Williamsburg, the capital of colonial America. Going over the Chesapeake Bay Bridge Tunnel, almost twelve miles long, was an awesome experience. In Charlottesville, we enjoyed visiting Thomas Jefferson's Monticello, a spacious and beautiful antebellum mansion celebrated for its architectural originality and colonial style. We also got a nice opportunity to travel and see parts of the southern USA.

During the colorful fall season, we used to take several trips to New Hampshire and Vermont to see the glorious "fall foliage". Those brilliant colors of purple, marigold, bright yellow, crimson and red unfolded in front of us for miles and miles, as far as the

130

eye could see. We loved the New England countryside for its unique natural beauty and peaceful atmosphere. Driving through those New England and New York highways, we often visited our friends Seema and Ram Chugh in Potsdam, in Upstate New York, near the Canadian border.

During one winter, we took a trip to see the Niagara Falls in Canada. On the return trip, we got caught in a huge snowstorm. The snow kept falling continuously for several hours. After a while, the driving conditions became very difficult and treacherous. In those days, I had a false sense of loyalty to a particular brand of gasoline, Mobil. (As I later realized, this was both misplaced and foolish.) It was partly the result of Mobil's persuasive and compelling advertising slogan, especially the phrase, "It cleans your engine as you drive." I should also add that my landlord in Norton, Mr. Arena, owned a Mobil gas station, and always used to harp on the superiority of Mobil gasoline. Even though the gasoline indicator was almost hitting the "empty" sign, I kept on driving, refusing to fill up the tank with any other brand besides Mobil. Mobil would have been proud to have such a pigheaded, loyal customer, I am sure. In fact, I passed up many such opportunities to buy another brand of gasoline, hoping that a Mobil station would soon show up. (Here, I must admit that I was absolutely naïve to cling to the idea of one brand of gasoline being superior to another—it is probably untrue—but I did not know, nor want to admit, any better at that time!)

Kamala was getting desperate and impatient with me. She kept chiding me for my apparent foolishness in sticking to one particular brand of gasoline (and misplaced loyalty, to be sure). I kept my cool, not wishing to make a bad situation worse. It was getting to be late in the evening. We had a hungry, restless toddler with us, crying for food. The bitter cold outside, coupled with the real prospect of being stranded on the highway, stared us in the face. There were very few cars on the road, and no help was at hand. It appeared as if very soon the gas tank would be completely empty. I started getting pretty nervous myself, though I hoped Kamala would be more patient and forgiving. Just in the nick of time, I saw

131

the flashing sign of a gas station in front of us. We barely made it to the pump. It was not a Mobil station. I was thankful to have any brand of gas, as long as it helped us to move to our destination in one piece. This experience taught me to get rid of my misguided loyalty to a particular consumer brand. I learned my lesson the hard way. It had been well learned, like many others, throughout my life!

Within a year, the college offered us a spacious apartment on the campus itself. It was nicknamed "The Sem." This was one of the residences owned by the college to house faculty members. It was a much-needed, welcome fringe benefit for me. We lived there until we left Norton in 1974.

Unlike Detroit, there were few Indian families in Norton or in its vicinity. Thus we were more or less isolated from the Indian community. Therefore, Tara and later Vidya, our second daughter, spent their childhoods without much direct contact with other Indian families. Whatever Indian culture they imbibed was mostly based on our home life.

Vidya was born on May 29, 1970, in nearby Sturdy Memorial Hospital in Attleboro. Until we left Norton in the summer of 1974, the children enjoyed playing in the company of several other kids of the Wheaton faculty. Our children's favorite companions were the Hippisley children. The Hippisleys were from Scotland. Prof. Hippisley taught Russian Language and literature. Whenever Kamala and I went for an evening's outing, our children were left with the Hippisleys. The other families with whom we grew very close were the Gonzalezes from Cuba, the Lubots from Oregon and the Walgreens from Mansfield, Massachusetts. Both the adults as well as the children of various faculty members delighted in each other's company. We had lots of good times and a great deal of fun. Norton was such a safe town that we often used to leave our doors unlocked, even when we were away from home for long periods of time.

Now for a couple of family health issues: Early in her childhood, Tara used to hold objects such as books and pictures very

132

close to her eyes. We did not think much about this for a while. In fact, every time she was holding something quite close to her eyes, I used to tell her to hold them farther away. It did not occur to me that she might have a vision problem. After several months of observing her persistent habit of holding objects so close to her eyes, it seemed a good idea to test her eyesight. At that time, she was barely three years old. We took her to the Eye Clinic at Massachusetts General Hospital in Boston. It turned out that Tara had acute congenital myopia. The ophthalmologist prescribed very thick, powerful lenses to correct her vision. She wore those glasses until she became a teenager. She was always self-conscious about her glasses. The doctor refused to prescribe contact lenses, stating that she was too young to wear them! During one of our visits to India, her grandfather (CRG) took her to an eye specialist, Dr. Jain, in Delhi, who prescribed corrective contact lenses for her. Tara was immensely happy to get rid of her thick glasses and grateful to her "Ampa" for helping her.

Vidya, too, happened to have a medical problem when she was a baby. We were not aware of it until Jim Wilmoth, our friend visiting from Michigan, pointed it out to us. (We are deeply grateful to him for this. It is always good to be frank and honest with friends, even if you think they might misunderstand you.) Her right foot and right leg were slightly twisted inward, making it difficult for her to crawl in a natural way. We suspected that she might be unable to walk normally as she got older. After consulting an orthopedic specialist, it was determined that she needed a cast on her foot. To straighten her twisted leg, it was necessary to put braces on both legs and hold them together with a metal instrument. She learned to crawl around the house with the cast in place all the time, except at night when she was sleeping. After several months of wearing it, the orthopedic problem was corrected and eventually she began to walk normally. We were greatly relieved to see the direction of her twisted feet change gradually; and happy that the problem was solved in her infancy.

The six years we spent in Norton passed away fast. Soon it was 1973. This turned out to be a watershed year in my professional life. It was the year I found out that I would not be tenured at Wheaton College. So I began looking for a job elsewhere.

It was a particularly difficult time for job seekers. Academic openings were few at that time. The American economy was going through a severe recession. Many research-oriented jobs (funded by federal money) and almost all government jobs were open only to citizens of the United States. It therefore seemed opportune to look for a suitable job abroad, especially in India. Going back to India (on a permanent basis) seemed like a viable option. We had lived for about ten years in America. I had already obtained my Ph.D. degree. When I left India, I had no idea that I would continue to stay here beyond the time needed to complete my studies. Besides, I had also gained six years of work experience. Our daughters were growing up fast. If we stayed here for a few more years, it would be even more difficult to go back and adapt to life in India thereafter. We had heard that some of the Indian families that had returned found the readjustment to Indian life extremely difficult. The longer one stayed in the United States, the harder it was to adjust to the rhythm of life in India. As we had not become American citizens, there was no compelling reason to stay here much longer. If we returned to India right away, we might be able to adjust and adapt without too much hardship.

Such thoughts were foremost in my mind when I started actively searching for a position in India's academic, research outfits or government agencies. I corresponded with several universities, research institutions and the UPSC (which was the recruiting arm for government jobs). I was prepared to go back on one condition: securing an appointment for a minimum of one year without the need for a prior personal interview. My reason for this stipulation was that I had not saved up much money during my stay in America, and could not afford to go back to India without a definite job offer in hand. Going back to India without securing a job for at least one year was not financially feasible. Nor could I afford to travel to India for a job interview at my own expense. That would have depleted my meager savings, without any guarantee that I could obtain a job there.

My job search proved unproductive, to say the least. Although some institutions expressed a lot of interest in hiring me, they would not make a definite job offer without a prior personal interview. Moreover, they were not prepared to provide travel funds for such an interview. This resulted in an impasse. After some futile negotiations, I decided to quit looking for a job in India.

It was then that Kamala and I started seriously thinking about becoming American citizens. Since we could not go back to India (with a job in hand), and many U.S. jobs that were being advertised did require U.S. citizenship, it seemed appropriate to become American citizens. Thus, purely economic and practical considerations dictated our decision to become citizens in this country.

Although at first we agonized about the wisdom of giving up our Indian citizenship, the employment situation was getting desperate. I did not have the luxury of waiting indefinitely to make a choice. To delay the citizenship decision much longer was not going to make the future any easier. After a few months of deliberation and hesitation, we decided to take the momentous step. There was no point in delaying action any further. We applied for U.S. citizenship in December 1973. After going through the necessary formalities, Kamala and I became U.S. citizens a year thereafter, in December 1974. The citizenship "swearing in" ceremony was held in Taunton, Massachusetts.

I reiterate that changing our Indian citizenship in order to become American citizens was a truly emotional experience for us. At first, giving up the Indian citizen identity seemed truly painful. We are all indelibly attached to our natal families and countries of birth. "Forsaking" the natural citizenship was not an unmixed blessing. But economic circumstances of the time, and the reality of the job situation, left very little scope for putting off this important decision. After we were sworn in as American citizens, we blended in very nicely with the growing population of naturalized citizens of our adopted land.

Meanwhile, my efforts to find a new job proved successful. I moved to William Paterson University in Wayne, New Jersey, as

135

Associate Professor of Economics in September 1974. Leaving Norton behind us was, indeed, a painful experience for our family. We have nostalgic and fond memories of the many good friendships we developed while living there. Our children, too, still cherish their early childhood years spent in that idyllic environment.

# Chapter 17

## Realizing the American Dream

When we moved from Norton to Wayne, we had very little money. Most of my savings were depleted in the summer of 1974 when I remained unemployed. Relocation expenses also absorbed a tidy part of these savings. My father-in-law (CRG) had come to stay with us while we were in Norton. This was his second visit to America. He retired from his government job in India in1973 and wanted to spend some time with our family. This gave Tara and Vidya an opportunity to bond with him in their early childhood. They called him "Ampa"—meaning mother's father. One of the disadvantages of living far away from one's kith and kin is that the younger generation does not get many chances to mingle with them. Our occasional visits to India did not give them sufficient time to develop close relationships with the extended family. I was glad that Ampa was in our midst for many months.

On one sunny September morning in 1974, we drove from Norton to Wayne. This was a distance of about 300 miles. It didn't take us very long to get settled in our new apartment in Wayne. The transition went on smoothly, except for Tara and Vidya. For quite a while, they missed their childhood friends in Norton. They still harbored nostalgic, fond memories of the people and places they left behind in Massachusetts.

Our new Wayne apartment seemed crowded compared to the spacious quarters we had in Norton. Tara and Vidya learned to share their room with Ampa. For them, the small playing fields in front of the new residence were a poor substitute for the vast meadows we left behind in Norton. But we all got used to our new surroundings in Byrne Court after a while. Within a few months, Kamala decided to continue with her studies. Her college education had been interrupted by our marriage in 1963. For more than ten years, she was content with her role as wife and mother. But now she was itching for new challenges and opportunities. With both children attending school, it was possible to resume her studies. She enrolled as a part-time student at William Paterson and started preparing for a degree in elementary/special education. Within three years, she completed all the required courses and obtained her B.Ed. in June 1978. Soon afterward, Kamala started her teaching career with the Franklin Lakes School system. She continued to teach there for the next twenty-two years.

The "college bug" seemed to have bitten her at this time. Not content with a bachelor's degree, she continued to attend school for five more years. In 1984, she completed her master's degree in education (summa cum laude). She excelled as a teacher in the classroom. As a committed teacher, she was popular with her students, their parents and the community alike. Her innate ability to teach and relate to young minds won her many awards, laurels and praise from several quarters. She was very happy in her role as a teacher and developer of young minds. I was extremely proud of her many professional accomplishments. Her selfless dedication to the cause of children's education was a model for all.

The large classes at William Paterson needed some adjustment in my teaching style. Having been used to the small-sized classes at Wheaton College, I found the new educational environment somewhat impersonal. It was difficult to get to know all the students by name. Some students made the comment that my academic standards were "very high and hard." Some of the students even complained to the dean that they thought I was teaching at the "graduate level." Initially, my teaching evaluations were not good. This was the first time in my teaching career that I found students doing "written evaluations" of teachers. At first, I did not like this practice at all. But there was nothing I could do about it. So I got used to it gradually. After a few semesters, I made appropriate adjustments in my teaching style and techniques. I tried to be as accommodating to the students' needs as I could, without compromising my own academic standards. Over time, such conscious adjustments in teaching and learning solved these problems.

I worked very hard to achieve several academic laurels. Besides teaching the standard undergraduate classes, I made innovative changes in the curriculum; introduced new honors courses; and continuously updated all my economics courses. A few years later, when we started the MBA program, I taught graduate courses and prepared grant applications. I was a member of various committees on campus, and played an important part in establishing the new School of Management within the university. In addition, I participated in scores of academic conferences held in the United States and abroad, presented several scholarly papers, and was a discussant and facilitator for many of them. A few of my papers were published in academic journals. I wrote articles for the local chamber of commerce, and was a consultant to small businesses and the local media. I did my best to impart economic education to the local business community by giving lectures at their gatherings. There were also rewarding opportunities to mingle with some local entrepreneurs and to get to know their problems and concerns, as well as help solve some of them.

Within five years after arriving at William Paterson, I was tenured in 1979. The following year, I was promoted as Professor of Economics. It was a dream come true in my professional life, and was certainly a watershed in my teaching career. Henceforth, I could devote my full energies in the pursuit of knowledge, as well as sharing that knowledge with others. Conferment of tenure by the university did give me the freedom to do whatever I wanted to do in my academic pursuits, without having to worry about job security. This was truly exhilarating, and I enjoyed this academic freedom to the fullest. My lifelong efforts to learn, teach others, and share my knowledge (and research efforts) with other scholars in the economics field provided that "ultimate fruit" I was searching for.

Early in 1980 we bought a house, even though the housing market at that time was very tight. As we had decided to set down roots in Wayne permanently, it seemed opportune to do so. The Byrne Court apartment was too small to accommodate our growing needs, especially the tiny kitchen. With the help of loans from three of our friends, we managed to scrape enough money for the requisite 20-pecent down payment on our property. The mortgage rate in those days was quite high—the lowest available rate was 9.5 percent, which we barely managed to get and qualify for. As both of us had stable jobs, we could afford the monthly mortgage payments, although it took a big chunk of our monthly income— almost 40 percent. In retrospect, the decision to purchase real estate at that time proved to be prescient. The property appreciated in value nicely over the next two decades. When we moved to Maryland after living in the Wayne house for nearly twenty years, it was worth almost four times its original purchase price of $96,000.

We lived in Wayne for over twenty-five years. This was the longest period we stayed in any one place during our entire lifetime. As homeowners, both Kamala and I became active in many civic and community activities. For a few years, I served on the Citizens Advisory Committee to the Wayne Board of Education. I was a member of the local chamber of commerce. We participated in fund-raising activities for several charities. As Friends of the Wayne Public Library, we were constantly helping with efforts to raise money for the library. Besides taking part in many such civic and community efforts to improve public life, they gave us ample scope to contribute our share of time and money to several worthy causes. Attending several public meetings of the Board of Education and participating in its deliberations was an enjoyable civic duty. As parents of two school-going children, we took every opportunity to influence public decision-making on the school budget, local taxation and government spending. As naturalized American citizens, it was an exciting experience to take part in the various local and national elections. We always tried to make full use of our rights and responsibilities as citizens of the republic. This was, for us, a proud and fulfilling part of living the "American Dream."

# Chapter 18

## Life as an Immigrant

When I came to the United States in 1963, my sole objective was to study here and thereafter return to India. At that time, I had no inkling that I would stay here permanently. After completing my Ph.D. in 1967, I had to stay back for a while in order to earn some money, even to buy my plane ticket. Returning to India immediately was not feasible since I did not have any funds to do so. Working here for a few years was the only practical way to save up funds for our eventual return.

With the birth of our children, six years passed before we could seriously entertain any thought of returning to India. In 1973, when we finally decided to return, my efforts to get a decent job in India did not succeed. I was deeply disappointed and frustrated by my fruitless job-hunting experience. Thus, my decision to stay back in the United States was the result of economic necessity. I had really no other alternative. The poor state of our family finances dictated my decision to stay permanently in the USA. Without a viable job offer from India, and absolutely no income or assets (property) to live there, I was forced to make the decision to become an immigrant.

In 1968, the U.S. Congress relaxed existing immigration rules and passed legislation enabling people from many developing countries to immigrate. The legislation was especially intended to encourage immigration of highly skilled people such as technical, scientific and engineering manpower. Eastern Hemisphere countries such as India were initially allowed an annual quota of 20,000 immigrants. Within a few years, the "family reunification" legislation also allowed close family members of U.S. citizens and permanent residents to immigrate. This added an open-ended number of persons to be qualified as new immigrants. India's annual quota was almost always over-subscribed. Indian immigrants, both skilled and unskilled, grew in size rapidly in the next two decades. By 1980 there was a sizeable population of Indian immigrants in many American cities. Some metropolitan areas such as New York, Chicago, Houston and Los Angeles boasted significant Indian immigrant communities. Over the years, these new immigrants continued to grow in size and influence. The New York-New Jersey metropolitan area was home to over 80,000 Indian immigrants by the year 1990.

This rapid influx of Indian immigrants resulted in the growth of a large Indian community in and around Wayne, as well as scores of other towns in New Jersey. This was in marked contrast with our earlier experience. When we moved to Wayne in 1974, our children had hardly any Indian classmates. The occasional Indian students with "brown skin" were dubbed as "Burnt Doritos"—as my daughter Vidya was nicknamed by her local white classmates. However, by the time she graduated from high school in 1987, there was a sizeable Indian immigrant student group in the Wayne School District, as well as other New Jersey school systems.

A couple of examples can illustrate the gulf that existed between the pre- and post-Indian immigrant era. When we came to the United States in 1963, the word "yogurt" was a novel one. It was probably unfamiliar to most average citizens in America. Even in New York City, the epitome of immigrant culture, we had a hard time locating an Indian restaurant or a grocery store selling Indian spices. One day, I was asked by an American on the street, "Where do you come from?" When I replied, "India," he immediately responded, "Is that in Egypt?" Although this was an extreme example of the average American's unfamiliarity with things Indian in the early 1960s, it illustrates the state of knowledge about India at that time.

There has been a sea of change since then. Now there are dozens of flavored yogurts sold in almost every supermarket in America. Fast food outlets selling spicy Indian *samosas* and other delicacies can be found on many street corners. Some big supermarket chains nowadays stock up selected items of Indian cuisine. Indian jewelry stores, movie houses and clothing stores have become familiar to the average American family. There are hundreds of stores in New York City doing a brisk business selling all sorts of goods made in India. Often it is difficult to get seating in an Indian restaurant there, especially on weekends, unless you make advance reservations. Celebrated Indian musician Ravi Shankar's sitar and percussionist Zakir Hussain's Tabla CDs can be found at Borders Music Stores and elsewhere.

It is not just Indian consumer goods and services that have become ubiquitous today. Many of the Indian writers in the English language (e.g. Bharati Mukerjee, Arundhati Roy, Salman Rushdie, Jhumpa Lahiri, Kiran Desai, Chitra Divakaruni, Vikram Seth and many others) are well known to readers throughout America. Indian art, paintings, sculpture and artifacts are prominently displayed in museums such as the Metropolitan in New York, Smithsonian in Washington, D.C., and the Museum of Fine Arts in Boston. Many universities and colleges offer courses in Indian Art, History, Languages and Culture. And there are some endowed chairs in Indian Civilization at some of these institutions. A surfeit of exhibitions and special shows depicting Indian history, art and architecture have had record-shattering patronage by the American public. It is also noteworthy that India's Republic Day and Diwali Holiday celebrations are occasions for large processions along Fifth Avenue in New York City. Mayors, local politicians and other public officials regularly attend them, just like other popular parades such as St. Patrick's Day and the Puerto Rican Festival.

The large number of Indian immigrant families in and around metropolitan areas and their suburbs has given rise to the growth of institutions catering to their distinct religious, cultural and linguistic heritage. One can observe many Indian youngsters, at the tender age of six or seven, learning classical music taught by dedicated practitioners of Carnatic and Hindustani systems of Indian music. Many Hindu temples, Moslem mosques and Sikh gurudwaras, dotted throughout the suburban landscape, impart religious instruction to these youngsters. Several schools teaching Bharatanatyam, Kuchipudi and Kathak styles of classical dance have had long waiting lists of eager students. These schools, some of which were origi-

143

nally started by well-known Indian dance teachers, have flourished in the last three decades. They have trained and graduated hundreds of budding young dancers, culminating in elaborate *arangetrams* (debuting performance) both in America and India. Several prominent Indian music teachers such as Ravi Shankar, Ali Akbar Khan, Alla Rakha and Zakir Hussain and their associates have established music schools in big cities such as New York, Los Angeles and Chicago. There are also now well-established annual music festivals celebrating the great composer Thyagaraja in cities such as Cleveland, New York and Washington, D.C.

Indian music associations in cities all over America regularly invite prominent musicians from India to perform several concerts and programs on a yearly basis. These are always well attended. The annual Carnatic music festival in Cleveland every Easter weekend attracts hundreds of music lovers from all over the Eastern United States and Canada. I have heard some people compare the Cleveland music event favorably with the celebrated Music Academy's festival in Chennai, India.

Such widespread cultural, religious and artistic activities help to keep alive and disseminate the rich traditions of Indian civilization to a wider American audience. This undoubtedly enhances international understanding and fosters greater inter-cultural exchange.

For over a decade (from 1990 to 2000), our family actively participated in the Northern New Jersey Music Lovers' annual festival. The daylong program gave an opportunity for youngsters, aged seven or eight and above to sing, dance and perform in competitive programs, showcasing their talents. Kamala was the master of ceremonies at several of these functions. She also was the emcee for a few Bharatanatyam arangetrams in New Jersey for many years.

We were both participants and spectators in this phenomenal growth of Indian immigrant communities in New Jersey and New York since the 1970s. Large numbers of immigrants from India's diverse linguistic and ethnic groups constitute a ready forum for

144

annual conferences in their respective languages. Today in America we have an annual meeting or conference for every conceivable religious, linguistic and regional group from India. Different Indian professional bodies such as associations of doctors, engineers, hotel and motel operators, software entrepreneurs, information technology personnel, nursing professionals, attorneys and real estate agents also have their own meetings and conferences every year. The list goes on, expanding and covering newer organizations and regions throughout the length and breadth of the United States and Canada.

As an economist, I have regularly attended the annual meetings of the Indian Economic Association held in various parts of the country. This was an occasion for Indian economists to get together and hold deliberations on the Indian economy year after year. Many of my associates looked forward to these annual gatherings not only for professional discussions but for renewing their personal contacts as well.

Many radio stations and TV programs today cater to Indian immigrants with different linguistic, ethnic and regional affiliations. Scores of magazines and newspapers, sometimes printed in India's distinct regional languages, can now be found in the roadside newsstands. Almost all such newspaper/magazine outlets are either owned or operated by immigrants from different parts of the world. And taxi drivers from the sub-continent are a familiar sight to anyone who has hired a cab in most metropolitan areas.

Indian yoga is all the rage in America today. Yoga centers, specializing in different schools and types of yoga abound everywhere. One can easily find a center representing a Chinmaya mission, a Ramakrishna mission or a particular Indian philosophical school, including the Dalai Lama. Of course a Hare Krishna center is not hard to find either in and around most big cities in America. Proponents of Indian yogic exercises, holistic healing practices and Hindu philosophy such as Deepak Chopra and Maharshi Mahesh Yogi have become very popular with both Indian and American followers.

145

Indian civilization and culture have permeated all facets of American life in the twenty-first century. People from India are to be found in all corners of this country. During the last forty years, a complete transformation has taken place in the average American's perception about India and things Indian. When Kamala came to Detroit in 1963, people used to stare at her walking around in a sari, wearing a bindi on her forehead. At that time, she was always wearing a sari, both at home as well as outside. Although many Indian women no longer walk around in a sari (most of them have adopted the Western style of clothing), many immigrants still habitually use their native costumes freely. Except for an occasional comment here and there, most Americans now accept many foreign costumes, food, languages, music, art and culture as their own. Gone are the days of wild stares and unsavory comments about things foreign and unfamiliar. It has now become easier and even fashionable to retain one's distinct cultural identity, without having to conform to the silent majority. The "melting pot" has given way to the "salad bowl," according to many social commentators. Multiculturalism is the new religion in America! And this new creed is actually being actively promoted with significant public funding throughout the land. We now have come full circle—from the exotic and unfamiliar to full integration and mainstreaming. Undoubtedly there has been a remarkable transformation in the nation's attitude and psyche about the distinction between what is foreign and American.

It is all too easy and convenient for many newly arriving Indian and other immigrants to adapt to life in America today. When immigrants first arrive to these shores, they generally tend to gravitate toward places and communities where earlier immigrants have settled. This makes the process of adaptation and acculturation much easier for newcomers. For them, being in the midst of a well-established, thriving immigrant community has distinct advantages. Having many of the familiar sights and sounds of one's native land in an otherwise alien (and sometimes hostile) setting is a great boon. People speaking one's native tongue and sharing familiar cultural values make for an easier life.

Such was not the case when I first arrived in 1963 in America. For some years, I was a cultural alien here. Although I was thoroughly familiar with American institutions and lifestyles, I did not feel that I had become fully assimilated to all aspects of American life. This is still true today in some aspects of living and thinking. Sometimes, I still wonder where I truly belong. Why is this?

The main problem has been my rural childhood background and upbringing. I have found it difficult to overcome some of the early ingrained habits and influences. My Kerala accent is one of these. The distinct intonation, in which the Malayalam language is spoken and heard, is completely different from that of English. My accent has a strong Keralite influence. Getting rid of that accent (with its emphasis on certain syllables and consonants) has been difficult for me, although some people are able to do it with comparative ease. During childhood, our tongues and jaws get used to saying some words and syllables in a particular way. Words in Malayalam require us to use our tongues and twist our vocal chords in ways that the English language does not. Therefore, the intonation, accent and style of speaking certain words of the English language are strongly influenced by the mother tongue and its peculiarities. The native language's influence, learned in early childhood, is very pronounced, and therefore difficult to get rid of. I have noticed that foreign-born celebrities such as Henry Kissinger and Sophia Loren are no exception to this accent-imposed "disadvantage."

Since language is our chief medium of communication with one another, I felt that my Kerala-heavy English accent was a distinct disadvantage in speaking "American English." No matter how slowly I speak the English language, some of the words I utter have a certain tinge of my native Malayalam in them. Years of living in America and trying to speak English "the American way" have not erased the early provincial influence of the native tongue.

To function successfully in a society different from the one you grew up in early childhood, we have to "unlearn" certain social skills and customs. To learn new skills and ways of thinking is sometimes easier than to forget old habits. Unless we are able to make this transition, everyday life becomes a little difficult. Most immigrants moving from one place to another face this problem. Adjustment and adaptation require strong commitment and motivation on our part.

As almost anyone can appreciate, new circumstances call for new skills and techniques to deal with life's challenges. Our ability to master the requisite knowledge and skills will determine whether we succeed or fail in everything life has to offer.

# Chapter 19

## A Flashback and Fast Forward

By its very nature, an autobiographical tome like mine is mostly written in chronological order. But it is impractical or inconvenient to write about all significant events in the exact order in which they took place. Rather than disturb the free-flowing style of the narrative to include many of the events in one's life that are worth writing about, it is more appropriate to bring them into focus as an aside. I have pulled together some of these themes in this chapter as a flashback.

When my father and mother passed away in 1982 and 1983, I could not go to Vilayur to be with my siblings to comfort them and be comforted. In most cultures across the world, marriages and deaths are customarily the occasions for family and friends to get together. We need to celebrate as well as to console in order to share our joys and sorrows. Marriages celebrate the joy of living, the coming together of two individuals as one entity. They are occasions for felicitation, feasting and fun. Death, on the other hand, is solemn. It forces us to evaluate our own life, its meaning and its purpose. The death of a loved one provides a unique opportunity for us to reflect on what we are doing with our own life. Bereaving the loss of the loved ones is the essential process of healing and hope for the future.

One of the big regrets I have had in life is that I could not attend the marriages of my siblings, except for my sister Thylam's in 1954. Nor could I share the pain of bereavement when my parents died. The most important reason for these lapses was distance, and also finance. The weddings took place after I left India in 1963. The expense of making frequent trips to attend weddings in India was considerable. Therefore I simply could not afford it. I had to be content with rejoicing in silence and solitude on those happy occasions when my brothers and sisters got married. Most weddings in India are arranged marriages. Traditionally, when sons get married, parents do not have to spend much money on them (unless they want to). But getting a daughter married is an altogether different matter. It imposes a big financial burden on most Indian parents. Despite the abolition of the dowry system in modern India, giving away a daughter in marriage still requires a lot of money. This is perhaps one of the reasons why boys are preferred to girls by many parents!

Helping with the funds needed for my sisters' marriages was the best contribution I could make toward my parents' financial wellbeing. Therefore, that is exactly what I did. It didn't matter much if I personally did not attend their marriages, but being able to contribute funds was extremely important. So, for conducting the marriages of my three sisters (Rajam, Annam and Kaveri), I helped my parents financially as much as I could. They depended on these financial contributions much more than my physical presence.

But I did want to attend at least one marriage of a family member. This opportunity came in December 2000. The occasion was the marriage of my niece Indira. I was overjoyed in being able to participate. My brother Ramakrishnan was especially glad to have me with him at his daughter's marriage, to felicitate the young couple. It felt good to be in the midst of the family. I realized then how much I had missed earlier. Kamala and my son-in-law Jamie were the ones who urged me to attend the wedding, despite some major obstacles. At first, I was somewhat hesitant to do so because we had planned a trip to India in another month, i.e., January 2001. But I was indeed happy to take their advice.

Since our arrival in the United States in 1963, our first visit to India was in the summer of 1966. Kamala's mother, Saroja, passed away in April 1966. At that time, we were unable to go. One of the "hazards" of living so far away is the difficulty of making frequent visits to India. This was especially the case for us in earlier years. For parents as well as children, these long absences (for several years at a time, as often happens) between infrequent family get-togethers can be traumatic. Kamala was deeply affected by her inability to see her mother after we left India.

150

This line of thinking was what prompted me to visit my parents in 1980. At that time, I had made up my mind to visit them without any further delay. A deep and persistent voice within me was urging me to make the trip. After some family discussion, Kamala decided to send Vidya along with me. This provided Vidya a chance to get to know her grandparents a little bit. During her two earlier visits to Vilayur in 1971 and 1975, she was simply too young to appreciate how life in my village was during my own childhood. I was determined to acquaint her with a semblance of those times.

Whenever he could, my father used to work on the family farm for several hours at a stretch. It was my job to carry jugs of tea for him. In those days he toiled extremely hard; nobody I knew worked harder than he did. I made it a point to take my daughter around the paddy fields of my childhood days. She could see how local farmers, working with farm animals and simple implements, cultivated rice. She could observe the rhythm of village life and its simplicity, a world completely different from the one she grew up with. I wanted her to see and experience a little bit of the old Vilayur that I had known when I was her age (in 1945). For her, looking at the various fruit trees like mangoes, cashews and banana, loaded with fruits was an exciting new experience. She could see how pepper and other spices grew on the vines creeping on the bigger trees in our compound. Vidya was fascinated to learn how we used to draw water from the well with a long rope and bucket. She tried it several times under my careful watch. It was interesting for me to observe how she communicated with her grandmother in broken Tamil (the language my mother spoke), punctuated with English words and idioms. I was equally fascinated with my role as translator and interpreter between them.

Watching her Thatha (grandfather) slicing green plantains to make delicious banana chips impressed Vidya a great deal. She observed him at work, doing different household chores, for hours together. She could also see him milking the cow every day in the morning. She was delighted when Thatha offered her a fresh glass of milk to drink, warm and delicious, straight from the source! He called upon one of the neighborhood boys to climb the tall coconut

151

tree and bring down a fresh coconut from the treetop. She watched excitedly as the boy started climbing up the tree with remarkable agility. He had a looped rope belt strung around his legs to facilitate the climb. He started going up and up the tree like a monkey (or rather a squirrel), and dropped a few coconuts to the ground, to be picked up by Vidya.

She was delighted and enthralled by this experience. Soon Thatha had husked the coconut with a hatchet or chopper in his hands, broke it open, and then poured out the sweet coconut milk (juice or sweet water) for his granddaughter to drink. The whole operation took less than ten minutes. Vidya had never seen anything like this in her life before. This was truly an eye-popping experience for her.

Visiting my aging parents in 1980 and spending some time with them was one of the best things I ever did. The timing of the visit was most appropriate too. They both passed away within a couple of years.

In the summer of 1985, we decided to visit my father-in-law (CRG) in India. We had planned to go with him on a Southern Indian tour. Two days after we arrived in Delhi, he suddenly died. We were fortunate to see him for a few hours in the hospital when he was still alive. During his previous visits to America, he had stayed with us for several months at a time. Tara and Vidya got to know him well when they were growing up. As a result, a deep bond developed between the grandfather and grandchildren.

Since we could not travel with CRG as we had planned, I wondered whether we should scrap the whole idea of traveling after he died. I thought about it for a while. During our previous visits, Tara and Vidya were too young to appreciate and understand the historical and cultural significance of India's great tourist attractions. Now was the right age when they could really enjoy such a trip. Another opportunity to do this might not occur for a long time, or ever, again. Therefore, I decided to seize the chance to take the family around for a three-week trip across the length and breadth of India. This was going to be one of the true highlights of

152

our life.

We had to make the best use of our limited time. To travel by train would have been an ideal way to see India, but it would take up too much of our time. We had seen some public television programs showing many interesting railroad journeys of the world. One of them was the great Indian Railways. Although a train journey through India would have been delightful, it had to be ruled out at this time because of time constraints.

So I went to the nearby office of the Indian Airlines to make inquiries about their "See India" plan. I consulted with their travel desk for several hours, and chalked out our itinerary. We planned our trip, keeping in mind the tight airline schedules. We had to make sure that we had enough time to see the most interesting and important places we wanted to visit. A feasible schedule was worked out, and I booked our flights right away. It suited our requirements very well.

The Dorai family enjoyed a wonderful tour for the next three weeks. It was packed with lots of fun, adventure, excitement and sight seeing. The journey began in Delhi and our first stop was Srinagar in Kashmir. On the first day, we took a bus tour of the city and its major attractions. After seeing the beautiful Dal Lake and Emperor Jehangir's famed Mughal Gardens, we took off to see the snow-capped mountains in the north. The entire route was picturesque. The road wound through many river valleys and peaceful villages where sparsely populated local tribes eked out a living by farming and sheep rearing. The entire route was lined on both sides with tall poplar, pine and other high-altitude conifer trees. The road wound its zigzag way through many mountain ranges, making sharp hairpin bends cut through them. The vistas on both sides were breathtaking to behold. Although it was the summer season, the air was getting very cold as we climbed to higher and higher elevations. Eventually we stopped for lunch at a rustic roadside kitchen run by one of the local tribesmen.

To observe the entire process of preparing the lunch, right from lighting of the hearth (a primitive oven), slicing of the raw vegetables, kneading the coarsely ground wheat flour and turning it into nice rounded fulkas (a local bread), was a novel experience for all of us. The cold open air was blowing on our faces while we stood around the open fire watching the entire cooking operation by the villager. Tara and Vidya had never before seen this kind of cooking done by a master chef. They were transfixed by the novelty of the cooking methods he used, their eyes glued on everything the cook was doing. The efficiency with which he was conducting the entire operation was really amazing. In about thirty minutes, a delicious lunch was readied for our starving stomachs. It was one of the best lunches we ever had. I couldn't believe that my children, who did not particularly care for Indian food, were asking for second and third servings of the *parattas* and vegetable curry and yogurt. They truly enjoyed their food that day.

The next stop on our trip was the village of Pahalgon. The place was beautiful beyond belief. Surrounded by tall mountain ranges all around, Pahalgon is situated in a deep, long valley. A fairly wide stream flows through the valley, full of crystal clear, cold water fed from the melting snow in the distant mountains. The entire village is situated on the banks of this beautiful river. Life in the village seems to revolve around the river. Sitting on the banks of the river and putting our feet in the cool, gently flowing stream was a very soothing experience. We did not want to move away from there. It is an especially favorite vacation spot where tourists come and stay throughout the year.

We bought a couple of woolen shawls and some small gift items in the nearby handicrafts emporium. We wanted to stay in Pahalgon longer, and would have certainly done so except that our bus was waiting for the return trip. This was indeed a place where one would like to go back again and again. I could see why since ancient times people have called Kashmir Valley one of the most beautiful places in the world.

On the third and last day of our Srinagar visit, I had an unpleasant experience. We started early in the morning on a long bus journey to visit many of the tourist attractions in the surrounding countryside. The bus was nearly filled with tourists like us, but in the back of the bus there were a couple of empty seats. One of the seats was partially torn, and it was wobbly and shaking. Since it was the only empty seat available, I sat on that seat. Throughout the trip, I had to hold on firmly to the seat in front of me to avoid falling down. After the trip was over, all the passengers got out of the bus one by one. For some strange reason that I could not fathom, the conductor went around the bus inspecting the seats. He found that the seat on which I was seated was wobbly and shaking, and was almost falling apart. He immediately accused me of having caused the damage and demanded a large sum of money as compensation. This outrageous demand infuriated me. I refused to pay, saying that the seat was already damaged before I sat on it. The conductor went on shouting at me, and insisted that he wouldn't let me go unless I paid him the money for damages. I got very angry and annoyed at this unexpected turn of events. I thought it was an unjustified attempt to extract money from an innocent passenger. A shouting scene ensued between the conductor and me. Ultimately I concluded that there was no point in arguing with this unreasonable man, and started my exit from the place in a hurry. The crowd of tourists, who had been watching the scene, gave me a big round of applause.

The next stop on our tour was Jaipur. The "pink city" was a delightful place to visit, with its colorful street scenery, exotic shops, its famous forts, palaces and many historical monuments. We made a round of the Amber Fort, took a camel ride, and visited Maharaja Jai Singh's Jantar Mantar. This was a collection of various geometrically shaped buildings and structures designed to measure the movement of the Sun's shadow at various times of the day. We spent a lot of time walking on the grounds and marveled at the ingenuity with which the Indian astronomers of the day (around 1620) had designed the buildings to achieve their measurement objectives.

From Jaipur, we proceeded to Udaipur and saw the famous Palace on the Lake. The palace seemed like a floating fantasy on Lake Pichola. Its long shadow, reflected in the clear waters of the lake during the moonlit night, was a unique sight to behold. The tourist guide who took us through the narrow mountain passes between the surrounding Aravalli hills told many stories of the fierce battles fought between the brave Rajput warriors and Emperor Akbar's invading armies. Many shrines were erected in the area honoring the great Rajput Kings who had died in battles defending their kingdom.

The next stop was a brief visit to Bombay (now renamed Mumbai) to visit my sister Annam and her family. Afterward, we proceeded to Aurangabad to visit the ancient Ellora Caves. Various stories and scenes from the Indian epics Ramayana and Mahabharata are depicted (etched and sculpted) on the walls of these caves. We learned that it took five generations of gifted sculptors more than 150 years to sculpt the stories from the Mahabharata on these cave walls. One can only marvel at the skill, effort and dedication with which those sculptors chiseled on these ancient rocks to carve such magnificent sculptures. We were overcome with awe and wonder as we gazed at these ingenious rock carvings.

Another adjacent cave complex was full of carvings too, dedicated to stories depicting the life of the Buddha and his disciples. A few miles beyond was a mosque called Bibi ki Mukbara, a prototype of the famous Taj Mahal in Agra.

We continued on the trip eastward, seeing many more thrilling architectural wonders in the temples at Belur and Halebid in Karnataka State. The colossal statue of Mahavira, the founder of Jainism (one of the religions that originated in India more than 2,500 years ago), was a thrill to behold. Carved on a great piece of rock on a hilltop, the statue can be seen from miles around. Climbing the hundreds of steps to reach the edifice and walking around the colossal structure was a breathtaking experience. More feast for our eyes awaited us at Mahabalipuram (near Chennai), a world heritage site where a complex of temples, all carved in stone, depicts various stories and legends from Indian mythology. These one-of-a-kind sculptures and carvings continue to attract large numbers of tourists from all over the world.

Next, we flew into Port Blair, the capital of the Andaman Islands in the Bay of Bengal. Here we stayed for a few days as guests of the governor and his family. We had a letter of introduction from Pandu, who was a friend of the governor. After a sumptuous dinner, our hosts took us for a cruise in the beautiful local harbor around dusk, just as the sun was setting on the distant horizon. The next day, we trekked through the dense tropical forests of teak and bamboo trees, and saw wild elephants roaming freely in the jungle. We saw large blocks of timber being cut; these were being hauled away by elephants for shipment to distant lands. The elephants were trained to pull the heavy loads through the jungle. To do the job, these great pachyderms, rather than trucks or tractors, were used because there were no roads there. Watching this operation was an experience unlike any other we had seen before.

Proceeding next to Puri, on the east coast of Orissa, we visited the ancient Jagannath Temple, one of the great holy Hindu shrines. The cool breeze of the sea helped to reduce the heat of the blazing midday sun. The temperature was around 110 degrees, even at 10 a.m. Undoubtedly, this was the place to construct a temple dedicated to the great Sun God. The Sun Temple at Konarak, the epitome of intricate ancient Indian architecture and sculpture, was an awesome sight in every way. It is hard to imagine how such life-like portrayals of everyday human activities (working, praying, eating, sleeping, fighting, making love, bathing, sleeping and many such mundane acts) can be depicted on stone with such clarity through the medium of sculpture. Our ancient forefathers were definitely consummate masters of this great craft. The Konarak Temple was definitely the place to spend a lot of time, walking around, reflecting, appreciating and enjoying this great masterpiece.

\* \* \*

NOTE: I was somewhat saddened by the poor state of repair in which these ancient gems of Indian sculpture, art and architecture had been kept. Centuries of willful neglect, natural erosion, vandalism and failure to maintain them properly have taken their toll. Many of these great treasures of our civilization have been irreparably damaged, and in some cases, defaced beyond repair. Belatedly, yet mercifully, the Archaeological Survey of India has taken steps to address these problems. It is heartening that they are now doing whatever is possible to secure the sites for future generations. I suppose lack of funding is a perennial obstacle in their mission. Many international agencies such as UNESCO are also spearheading efforts to restore these sites for the enjoyment of posterity.

* * *

We were soon headed for the last leg of our historic journey. We rounded out our trip with a visit to Varanasi. There we saw the Burial Ghats on the river Ganges as well as the temple of Mahadeva, which millions of Hindus consider as one of their most sacred religious shrines. Moving on to Agra, we visited the celebrated Taj Mahal, the Agra Fort and Emperor Akbar's capital city of Fatehpur Sikri. So much history, art, architectural glory and natural scenery were packed into our mini-discovery-of-India trip over three weeks. The scope, grandeur and splendor of it all overwhelmed us.

The time, energy and money spent on the trip gave our family a truly unforgettable lifetime experience. It whetted our appetite for travel. The memory of that journey is forever etched in our psyches.

Tara started her college education in 1983 at the University of Delaware, after graduating from Wayne Hills High School. She decided to major in International Relations. During her college days, she met Jon Berry, who was studying Electrical Engineering. They dated, fell in love and continued a long-time love relationship.

My feelings when I first met Jon were somewhat mixed. With his disheveled hair flowing toward his shoulders and a thoroughly soft-spoken demeanor, he initially appeared to me like one of those "hippies." I was quite unprepared to entertain thoughts about Jon as my future son-in-law. One has to unlearn a lot before one can learn anew. Our notions about what is right and proper change over time as we are exposed to new ideas and experiences. Many a time, first impressions and opinions can be very deceptive, and indeed, often turn out to be such. I was no exception to this maxim. Soon, I had to learn to accept Jon as a member of our family. It took me several months before I could have meaningful conversations with him. I gradually got used to his presence on weekends and holidays, whenever Tara chose to bring him along to our home in Wayne. On a few occasions, we took them to New York to visit various museums and have leisurely dinners at the Bombay Palace restaurant (a favorite eating place for them). Jon immediately took a liking to Indian food, and always enjoyed Kamala's delicious *Alu Parattas* and other home-cooked delicacies. In fact, he would be disappointed if we did not prepare spicy Indian dishes during his visits. He also picked up a few words of Tamil from Tara, and surprised us with his familiarity with Indian culture. He made a sincere effort to blend in with our family values. I was equally impressed by the depth of his knowledge and pleased by his well-rounded education.

During her college years (1983-87), Tara brought Jon to our home many times. He also met Ampa (CRG) during one of those visits. Ampa and Jon struck a good rapport immediately. Gradually, we were introduced to Jon's parents, Jon Berry Sr. and Jan. We developed a growing friendship with them as the years rolled by. Upon graduation in 1987, both Tara and Jon moved to an apartment in Owings Mills near Baltimore.

In 1990 when Tara was ready to marry Jon, we asked her what kind of wedding ceremony she wanted to have. We were willing to celebrate the wedding in any manner Tara chose. Tara indicated that she preferred to have a full Hindu wedding ceremony, with all the traditional rituals. She had seen some Indian wedding movies and videos, and she thought it would be nice to have such a wedding ceremony. Jon was fascinated by the idea of having a *Kashi Yatra* (a visit to Holy Banares, as he called it), which is an integral part of many traditional South Indian (especially Brahmin) wedding ceremonies.

\* \* \*

159

NOTE: This antiquated, somewhat bizarre ritual has some special meaning and significance. It symbolizes a sudden "misgiving" by the prospective bridegroom about the wisdom of getting married to his chosen bride. He shows a sudden reluctance (shall we say, hesitation) to proceed with the impending marriage. He half-heartedly takes a few steps toward the holy city of Kashi, rejecting the idea of marriage and preferring instead the life of a bachelor. Thereupon, the father of the bride follows the reluctant bachelor and persuades him to return and marry the beautiful, accomplished daughter. The prospective bridegroom is at last convinced about the merits of matrimony. The father succeeds in his mission, and the bridegroom is happy to proceed with the marriage ceremony.

* * *

Tara and Jon meticulously planned all the fine details of the wedding ceremony and the subsequent reception. We obtained the services of a Hindu priest, and fixed April 8, 1990, for the ceremony.

In many ways, Kamala and I were pioneer Indian immigrants. Because we came to America in 1963 when there were very few Indian families here, we did not have the benefit of many established traditions to follow or guide us. Our children were born and raised a few years ahead of most other children born to Indian immigrant parents. In conducting the marriage of our daughter, we decided to do what we thought was "our way of doing things." From India, Kamala's sisters, Prema and Usha, along with her husband, Pandu, came to attend the wedding. Some of the rituals of the wedding ceremony were improvised or modified to suit local conditions. For example, we put together a "hibachi" platform for conducting the Vedic Homam (offering salutations and seeking the blessings of Agni) and to perform the "Saptapati," the seven steps necessary for a mutually harmonious and happy married life. Such innovations and modifications were done to make the ceremony simpler and more practical, while retaining its essential core principles. We also prepared and distributed a small pamphlet explaining the meaning and significance of these steps (customs) so that the audience could understand what was going on.

160

The learned Pundit Agnihotri (Hindu Priest) who conducted the wedding rites hailed from a family of Brahmin priests in the Gujarat State of India. We learned that his grandfather was a well-known and highly respected scholar priest there. While conducting the marriage, the Pundit would initially chant the appropriate mantra (sloka or verse) in Sanskrit, and then translate its meaning into English for the benefit of the assembled guests. This made the ceremony very lively and interesting for all.

Vidya, too, self-selected her spouse soon after her graduation from the University of Maryland. Her life partner, Ronald James Ambrosi (whom we call Jamie), is the descendent of Italian immigrants who came to the United States during the early part of the twentieth century. After graduating from college in 1992, Vidya decided to pursue a career in education. Subsequently she got a master's degree in Education from Towson University and started her career as an elementary school teacher. She decided to celebrate her marriage with Jamie in June 1996.

Her wedding with Jamie took place on June 15, 1996, in a splendid outdoor setting on the grounds of Franklin Lakes Country Club. It was a really colorful ceremony. Vidya and Jamie wanted a simple Christian ceremony, followed by a traditional Hindu wedding. Both ceremonies took place in the outdoors on a perfect summer afternoon against the backdrop of the glorious sun shedding its golden rays on the shimmering waters of the lake in the background.

According to ancient Indian traditions and culture, Kamala and I felt that we had discharged our parental responsibilities in a fitting manner. Both of our daughters were now free to pursue their own aspirations in life. Having been born and brought up in America, they had been given a good education and a decent start in life. We had done our best to bring them up as good citizens and responsible members of society. We felt a sense of pride and joy in doing this successfully. Our promise to each other during the Saptapati was fulfilled. Our daughters were now ready and eager to pursue their own future lives with their spouses. This was a dream come true.

# Chapter 20

## A Brush with Death

Sometime during 1979 I went for a complete medical checkup. My blood sugar at that time was high. I was diagnosed as a diabetic. For several years, I tried to control the diabetic condition with diet and regular exercise. One day, in May 1990, I started feeling very dizzy and tired. When I checked with the doctor, it was found that my blood sugar was around 360, a highly elevated level. Immediately thereafter, I was put on medication and a strict diet to control the blood sugar. I have been on diabetic medication since that time.

On April 8, 1999, we celebrated the first birthday of our granddaughter Aarthi in New Jersey. After the birthday party, all the family members, including Kamala, returned to Maryland. I was staying alone in Wayne.

The next day, I was working at the college as usual. A faculty meeting was scheduled on that afternoon. There was a discussion going on at the meeting. I was sitting in my chair, waiting for my turn to speak.

Suddenly I fell down from my chair, unconscious. I do not know what happened, except that when I woke up, people were hovering around me, trying to resuscitate me. It appears that when I fell down, I had hit the floor, causing a small wound on my forehead. I was bleeding. I regained my consciousness within a few minutes. The ambulance was called, and they rushed me to Wayne General Hospital. I was in the Emergency Room for about four hours. They did various tests on me to determine the cause of my fall. The cardiologist, Dr. Das, informed me that my heart was not beating properly, and that I needed a pacemaker. I was told that I needed to stay in the hospital and surgery was required to implant the pacemaker.

I found it hard to believe what was being said about my heart

163

condition. At first I protested in disbelief and told Dr. Das that I wanted to go home. I thought it was unnecessary to implant a pacemaker, as I felt quite normal at that time. Dr. Das, however, insisted that I should stay in the hospital, and that going home in my present condition (without Kamala being at home) was not advisable. In fact, he would not permit it. He said that if I insisted on going home, I would have to go to "his home," where he could keep an eye on me!

This was pretty serious stuff. I started ruminating about my situation. I thought, mistakenly, that the whole thing was a cruel joke. I thought it would be a good idea to spend my time in the emergency room writing my will. I had not prepared this important document before. Suddenly, I realized that if I were to die soon, my wife would be left without a will.

I had brought no papers with me when the ambulance rushed me to the hospital. Therefore, I asked the nurse to give me a piece of paper to write my will. Right away, I started hastily putting together my last will and testament. I wrote a few clear instructions for Kamala to follow in the event of my death. I requested the attending nurse to witness the document.

That evening I was admitted to the cardiac intensive care unit. I was scheduled for a pacemaker implantation the next afternoon. During the night, my condition worsened. Around 10 p.m., my heartbeat started falling. I had again lost consciousness. When I awoke, I realized that something strange was happening in my head. The nurse said that I needed oxygen. An artificial respirator was attached to my nose. I breathed normally for a while.

Again, after some time, it seemed to me that I was floating somewhere. The vigilant nurse who was by my side informed me that what I was going through was the result of the heart not being able to do its job. The nurse put me on an external pacemaker to normalize my heartbeat. It seemed that my heart was not functioning as it should. Dr. Das was absolutely right. I would have died if I went home that night. He had saved my life.

The next morning, I requested Dr. Das to call Kamala and in-

164

form her about what happened. By the time Kamala arrived around 3 p.m., the pacemaker had been implanted. The surgery went smoothly. I was now recovering well.

At the hospital, many random thoughts were going through my mind one after another. I began to reflect on my life and how I had lived. It was a good time to take stock of what I had done with my life. I reviewed my past.

It seemed to me that I had done many of the things I wanted to do. My life had taken the direction I wanted it to take. A long time back, I had made a conscious decision to educate myself, learn and teach. This I was able to do. I had married the woman I loved. We had a happy and productive life together. We raised two good children and tried to teach them the important values we cherished. We provided them with the kind of college education they wanted, and which we could afford. We had taught them important life skills so that they could henceforth manage their adult lives.

Probably, the chief concern I had for many years was whether Kamala, Tara and Vidya would be able to manage their lives in my absence. My solemn responsibility, I knew all along, was to equip them with the necessary education and skills to make a living on their own. It was a great relief to realize that Kamala, since the time she graduated in 1978, was able to earn and become financially self-sufficient. That she could have managed on her own, without me, was certain, though with some hardship. Kamala was a resourceful individual, full of energy and many talents. In many ways, she was much more "street smart" than I was. I wanted to ensure the same for Tara and Vidya. The best means to achieve this goal was to give them a good education. Since that was already accomplished, I was content and at peace with myself.

To realize that my wife and children were well established was a joyful thought. I did not have to worry about them any more.

I had helped my parents as much as I could when they were alive. I was a good son; to my siblings too, I was a good brother. I had done my very best for many members of my extended family.

I studied what I wanted; I learned well; I worked in an occupation I enjoyed; I earned a decent income; I served society to the best of my ability. I knew I was an asset to my community, and a good citizen of the world.

With this realization, now I could die in peace.

A PHILOSOPHICAL FOOTNOTE:

Steeped in the ancient moral and religious traditions of India, I had learned in my formative years that the four important goals of our lives were:

1. "Dharma" (first and foremost, and above all else, doing what is right, under all circumstances; doing one's duty)

2. "Artha" (earning money; creating wealth; reaching financial independence; attaining material prosperity)

3. "Kama" (satisfying all our sensual urges, and fulfilling our desires)

4. "Moksha" (salvation; nirvana: ultimate spiritual freedom)

These noble missions (goals) of the good life were my guidelines throughout life. I must confess, however, that I did not consciously think about them always. Invisibly and lurking in the unconscious mind, they were nevertheless propelling me into action.

What more can one expect from life? If you are able to get what you yearn for, isn't that what fulfillment is all about?

I realized then that I had lived "the good life." I had done almost everything I wanted to do. I was certainly ready for the journey ahead.

These ruminations aside, I recovered from my ordeal and went home. I had a new appreciation of life. What happens from now onward is a bonus, isn't it?

# Chapter 21

## The Move to Baltimore

Thoughts of retiring from work had not really entered my mind as yet (in 1999). No doubt there was some vague, occasional discussion about where we might go if and when we retired at some future time. When we were visiting San Antonio some time back, the layout of the city and its ambience had charmed us. It was a relatively nice, clean, small city. The climate was warm throughout the year. The small river running right through the middle of the city, with many charming restaurants and sidewalk shops on its banks, looked enchanting. The city had a good library, and a university. It was very cosmopolitan. These were the attributes we would have liked in an ideal retirement community. Living during retirement in one of the many beautiful small houses built on the riverside was an appealing thought. The city's multi-ethnic character had much to recommend it. I had tucked away these thoughts in the back of my mind then.

Another likely retirement choice was close to our hometown. We used to drive through Princeton a lot. Whenever we were visiting our friends Viji and Sudarsanam in Hamilton, we often went through Princeton Township. It too seemed like a nice place to retire. Princeton had all the desirable features we were looking for in a retirement community, such as: a good library, a university, many cultural events, sports facilities, good ambience, friends close by and proximity to a large metropolis (New York).

Such thoughts about where we might want to retire and when that might happen seemed like sheer fantasy at that time. I had no serious thoughts about retirement for many more years. I had a good job. I had lots of accumulated debts to repay. Our mortgage was not going to be paid off until another ten years or so. We still needed to wait a few more years before we could accumulate enough money in our retirement plans (funds). Kamala would not

167

be eligible to draw a pension until she completed at least twenty-five years on the job. Her health benefits would not be vested until then. This target date would have been 2005, at the earliest.

Since 1992, we were frequently traveling to Owings Mills, near Baltimore, to visit our grandson Niklas. He was born on September 9, 1992, which was the day of our twenty-ninth wedding anniversary. Tara and Jon had been making occasional trips to Wayne to visit us after their marriage in April 1990, until their son Niklas was born. With a small baby in their hands, these visits became more problematic as time went on. Both Tara and Jon had full-time jobs. They found it difficult to come to Wayne often to see us. It seemed more convenient for us to get into our car and make the four-hour trip to Baltimore as often as we wanted to do. We did these trips more and more frequently. After Tara and Jon's second son Kristofer's birth in December 1995, we found ourselves visiting the grandchildren once a fortnight or sometimes once every three weeks.

When Vidya and Jamie got married in June 1996, they too decided to live near Baltimore. After visiting Tara in Owings Mills, we would make a side trip to Vidya's place in Germantown. In 1997 they had moved to Germantown near their place of employment. After their daughter Aarthi's birth in April 1998, we found ourselves going to Germantown for fortnightly visits. The drive from Wayne to Germantown would take almost five hours on the busy Interstate 80 through the Pennsylvania countryside. We would usually start these trips on Friday evenings, reaching Germantown by about 10 p.m. The return trip had to be planned for Sunday afternoons so that we could come back to Wayne before Sunday evenings. Both Kamala and I had to get back to work on Monday mornings.

These weekend trips to visit Tara and Vidya became very tiresome and time-consuming. They were exhausting and sapped our energy a great deal. We realized that we were spending too much time on the road driving to and fro. It was no longer feasible to combine our trips to visit both children (into one trip) as we used to do earlier. Though we wanted to see our grandchildren often, the

168

prospect of sitting in congested traffic on the busy highways became less and less appealing. During our journeys, Kamala and I wondered how long we could continue to make these road trips. But there were no other viable alternatives (or means of transportation) if we wanted to visit our families frequently.

Gradually, we started some serious discussion about our eventual retirement prospects while traveling in the car. After my sudden and unexpected "brush with death," we became more and more conscious of our limited life span. Kamala was getting frustrated with her teaching job as well. A newly appointed principal seemed to be making her job less and less enjoyable. Roy Egatz, her old principal, was a boss with a laid-back style who gave teachers lots of freedom and initiative in teaching their classes. He always encouraged his staff to be creative, independent and innovative. Kamala was used to his style of supervision and had enjoyed working with him for almost seventeen years. When he retired in 1996, the new principal who took Roy's place came with a completely different management style and attitude toward the teaching staff.

The new principal tried to impose her intrusive, bossy and micro-management style on the teachers. Kamala found it very difficult to work with the new boss. She constantly complained about the deteriorating work environment in the school. She was always telling me how difficult it was to work with the new administration. The great joy of interacting with her classroom, the spontaneity, the creativity and the sheer pleasure of teaching young kids— the hallmarks of her professional life—were missing. She no longer looked forward eagerly every morning to going to work. The old spark and unbridled enthusiasm were somehow missing. Going to school started becoming almost like an invisible torture, an unpleasant chore, no longer satisfying like the "good old days."

In these circumstances, Kamala wanted to quit her job before reaching the normal retirement age of sixty. That would have been in 2005. The question we faced right now was, could we afford to retire sooner—in 1999?

Was it at all feasible financially? Or even desirable? If we decided to retire right away, we knew it would turn out to be an irrevocable decision. So, one day, we sat down and started talking seriously about it. There was an air of urgency in our discussions. The conversation went on as follows:

Kamala: "Let us talk about what has been bugging me about my job. It is becoming very difficult for me to work in the school these days. You know I have been coming back every day with severe headaches. At this rate, I don't think I will be able to continue in that school for long. Can I quit now? What do you think? Can we manage with just one salary? Yours? Or should we both retire together? That would be perfect if we could do so. There are pluses and minuses, no matter what we do. Let us explore this. Tell me what you think."

Gopal: "Of course. If you quit, I think we can probably manage. Didn't we live on one salary for many years? You started working only less than twenty years ago. We certainly managed until about 1979 with my salary. Did we not? It is not a question of being able to manage. There are many other things to think about before retiring. It is not like quitting one job and taking up another one. Once we retire, we probably cannot get another job. We may not even want to work again. We have to say goodbye to the working life once and for all. We must also decide where to live. What should we do with our house? What are we going to do with our spare time? How should we spend our retirement years? These issues have to be discussed. Of course, if you want, you can retire. There is no problem with that."

Kamala: "I know. I have been thinking a lot. We have to discuss all these issues carefully. Do you think both of us can retire together? It will be boring for me to stay home when you continue to work. Not only that, I want to see our children and grandchildren as much as possible, and help them when we can do so. You know, these weekend drives to Baltimore are becoming extremely difficult. We cannot really continue to do this. If you continue to work and I quit, this problem is still going to be there. How are we going to deal with that?"

170

Gopal: "Precisely. It seems to me that there are many advantages in both of us quitting our work together. We will both be free to do whatever we want, whenever we want. I don't have to be tied down to my college schedule. I have to make some calculations and see whether we can both retire together. Suppose we do that, then what? If we continue to live in our Wayne house, we will still need to drive to Baltimore to see the kids. How long do we want to stay with them each time we go there? Is that going to be feasible? Would they like that? How often should we go to see them?"

Kamala: "I certainly would like you to retire too, when I retire. Then we can do what we want, when we want. That would be nice. Can we do that?"

Gopal: "Let me see. I will check this out and then tell you. But we still have to discuss the problem of what to do with our house. Shall we continue to live here? Or do we go to someplace like Princeton or San Antonio, or some other place? The place to which we ultimately retire is very important. It must have all the amenities that we want."

Kamala: "I really like to be near the ocean. I like water. I would like to have a house close to the water, say near a lake. I enjoy looking at the water."

Gopal: "That is going to be difficult. Any place near the water is going to be very expensive. Where will that be? On the New Jersey Shore? Or some other place? We still have to deal with the problem of how to see the kids, I mean, transportation. If we relocate to some other place, isn't the question of driving going to be there?"

Kamala: "I suppose so. I guess I am just dreaming when I say I want to be near the water. You are probably right. We really should move to a place near the kids. Then we will not have a driving problem. We are both getting old. We cannot think of being too far away from the children."

Gopal: "Suppose we both decide to retire. Shall we continue to live in Wayne, and go to Baltimore occasionally, whenever we

171

choose? We will no longer have to confine our trips to the weekends and holidays. First and foremost, we have to decide on this."

Kamala: "I really don't want to live in this house after we retire. I want to go away from here. I just don't like this place. We should sell this house and move away. We should look for a suitable house in some other place."

Gopal: "Where? Whatever money we get by selling this house will have to be spent on buying a new house. House prices in most places have gone up."

Kamala: "Then let us decide to move and buy a new house somewhere. I always wanted a new house. I am tired of old houses, old furniture, old car, and old stuff. I want to have a new one, just once in my life. Let us move closer to the kids and start looking for a house there. If I cannot get a new house, I will probably settle for an old house, as long as I can remodel it the way I want."

Gopal: "Then we have to go and start looking. It is going to be tough. We have to think about putting our Wayne house on the market. The retirement decision and house-buying decision are tied together. We really cannot do one without the other."

Kamala: "Next time we go to the kids, let us talk to them. Perhaps we should see a real estate agent and find out the housing situation there. Let us explore. I definitely think we both should retire together and move away from Wayne. Let us go and find a place near the kids. That would solve our problems."

Gopal: "What about your pension and health benefits? Are you really prepared to give up your health benefits? It is a very important issue, you know. Health care is becoming very expensive. If you held on to your job for another three years, we will get free health benefits for life. I will be covered under your plan. If we retire now, my health benefits plan is not very good. I will have to pay premiums every month. You will be covered under my plan, no doubt, but it is uncertain what the monthly premiums would be. Our union has not been able to negotiate a good health plan from the State."

Kamala: "I know exactly what you are saying. This is the one thing I worry about all the time. But what is the use of having a good health benefits plan but poor health? I think if I continue in my job, I will be dead before five years."

Gopal: "I understand. I agree with you. We will somehow manage with my health plan. We may also have to spend money from our pocket in addition to the health plan. But I don't want you to say later that I didn't warn you beforehand about these issues. Once we both retire, and you are put on my health plan, our monthly premium may jump a lot. Health care expenses are going through the roof. We will be faced with increasing health care costs. Myself being a diabetic, and with your history of health problems, we will have to be very careful."

Kamala: "I think we should discuss our plans with Tara and Vidya when we go there next. We should tell the kids. Let us explore the housing situation there. Then let us put our house up for sale. As I said, we should move close to the kids. Please find out whether we can both retire together next year. Then we will give notice to our employers. I think that would be the best thing."

Gopal: "All right. I will think about this carefully. Then we will decide. I think we can manage somehow if we are careful. We should be able to find a reasonably priced house near the kids. If we are able to sell our Wayne house before we commit ourselves to a house in Baltimore, we should be all right. We don't want to have to carry two mortgages together. That would be impossible. I want to make sure we sell our house here before we commit ourselves to a house and a new mortgage. What do you think?"

Kamala: "Absolutely. Let us do it. There is no point in postponing the decision any longer. Let us do what we have to do. Even if we move to an apartment for a while, I don't mind. No way can we afford to have two payments. I know that."

Gopal: "Then here is my strategy. After looking at all the pros and cons carefully, we will give notice to our employers that we will retire in June 2000. Then we will put our house up for sale. After selling it, we will think about buying a new house somewhere near the kids. What do you think? Is that okay?"

Kamala: "Yes, fine. As long as I don't have to work after next year, I will be happy. If I know for sure that I am quitting my job, one more year won't be so bad. I can certainly manage for another year. It is the thought about five more years that gives me the creeps. I can't stick around in my job for that long."

Gopal: "All right. We will do it. I think we have discussed most of the important issues. Let us have a good cup of coffee."

It didn't take me long after our conversation to make our final decision. After looking into the pros and cons of retiring in 2000, I came to the conclusion that it was indeed feasible. With careful management of our finances, we could afford to retire now. Until Kamala started getting her own pension in 2005, we could be quite comfortable with my retirement income, so we notified our employers that we intended to retire at the end of the 1999-2000 academic year.

This was a momentous decision for us. Having cleared my mind about all the issues surrounding the retirement decision, I was ready to say goodbye to almost forty years of my academic career.

The next step was to sell our Wayne house and move to a place somewhere in the vicinity of the children.

During our many succeeding trips to Baltimore, we looked at various houses available on the market. We had to make sure that its possible purchase price was somewhere in the neighborhood of what our Wayne house might sell for. We had our house appraised by a couple of real estate agents. They thought we might be able to sell the house for about $350,000.

Armed with this information, we were on the lookout for a suitable property somewhere near Tara/Vidya's neighborhood. Many of the houses we looked at were too expensive; inconveniently located; too old, needing extensive repairs; or did not fit our specifications in other ways.

One day, in November 1999, driving on the Baltimore Pike in

174

Ellicott City, we happened to see a billboard announcing the availability of new villas being built on Turf Valley Road. The advertised price seemed to be reasonable, and in our mental price range. We decided to take a careful look at the place. We drove to the sales office, and made enquiries.

The location of the villas seemed ideal. They were being built with most of the amenities we wanted. The price, too, was about right: close to $360,000. One hitch might be the possible delay in completing the construction. We were told that the construction would be completed by June or July 2000, and the house could be ready for occupation sometime in the late summer months, probably around August or September.

We decided to put down the requisite initial deposit. We signed the final contract to purchase the house in February 2000. We then knew that we had to make arrangements to sell our Wayne house right away, so that all the funds needed to buy the new property would be available in time.

To our surprise and utter delight, we sold our house within a week.

We got the price we asked, which was close to the appraised value. Apparently the real estate market in metropolitan areas like Wayne and Baltimore was hot. We had to move out of our house before the end of March 2000. The new owners wanted to move in right away.

After some search, we found a temporary furnished apartment in Wayne, not far from our old house. Some of the furnishings and personal effects we wanted to keep were put in storage for a few months until we were ready to move to Baltimore. A substantial part of the old furnishings, clothing, books, paintings, artifacts and many other items were donated to the Salvation Army or given to neighbors. A few items were sold for whatever they could fetch. A lot of stuff was thrown away. I realized how many material things we had accumulated over thirty-seven years, since we set foot on American soil. I was glad to donate a large part of my personal library collection to William Paterson University.

175

We stayed in the rented apartment for about three months. To live there, in a one-bedroom unit with a small "efficiency kitchen," was quite a change from our old house. Living there felt like our graduate school days. We actually enjoyed the experience. Once again, we felt free from the responsibilities of owning a home. It was good while it lasted, to say the least. For a while, we didn't have to worry about the mundane chores of cleaning the place, cutting the lawn, taking care of a garden and other jobs associated with home ownership. It was a welcome relief from what we had been doing for the last two decades. It was almost like the "good old Detroit days" of our early married life.

Soon, June 26, 2000, arrived. This was the last day of teaching for Kamala. Her academic career would soon end. A few days earlier, her school colleagues and staff had given her a grand retirement party.

Earlier, I had already packed my books and some important academic papers in my office at the university. A few days before that, the university had held a memorable retirement party for the three professors who were retiring along with me. In my farewell remarks, it was really hard for me to say goodbye to my students and colleagues. So much of my professional life, and the happy memories associated with it, had been spent at the university.

Packing the few clothing and books we had brought to the temporary apartment, we got into our cars and started driving to Vidya's house in Germantown. We reached there late at night. This was the last day of our teaching careers. And it marked the beginning of our "Golden Years" in retirement. We were sad, but also excited about the life ahead of us.

# Chapter 22

## Life in Retirement

The first six months of our retired life, from June to December 2000, were spent in Vidya's household while our new home was being built. Though the builder had promised us that the house would be ready by July or August, many unexpected construction delays occurred, so we continued to stay in our daughter's home. We now had to make two kinds of psychological adjustments: first, getting used to a "non-working" retired mode; and second, becoming attuned to living in somewhat cramped quarters with our daughter's family.

For me, the first of these adjustment problems was rather hard at first. Having been used to a busy work schedule for almost fifty years, the new "freedom from work" seemed painfully difficult. I spent my time helping with the family chores. I took long walks. I frequented the local library and read many books. I visited the chamber of commerce office to learn about new business opportunities. I played a lot of tennis. I looked into our personal finances carefully. I tinkered with my investments to make sure they were performing as expected. I reallocated my portfolio, and for a while did some modest stock trading. I corresponded a lot with friends and family members in India. Kamala and I spent some time touring California and Canada (which we had planned to do earlier, before leaving Wayne). And we also made frequent visits to our future home to monitor the building's progress.

At last, we signed our mortgage papers and moved into our new living quarters in Ellicott City in December 2000. There was much to do for the next few months: buying new furniture, establishing new banking/insurance relationships, transferring medical records and papers to new service providers, and myriad other chores associated with the change of residence. These tasks absorbed a lot of time and energy. We also visited India for a period of roughly three months. We traveled extensively, met with various family members and friends, and attended some weddings.

With these activities now behind me, I began to wonder how best to spend my retirement years. There were several conflicting, but also complementary goals:

To spend time with grandchildren and take part in family and children's school activities. (I have been able to devote much more time to my two youngest grandkids, Anand and Anil, than I could with the older ones (Niklas, Kristofer and Aarthi) when I was in New Jersey).

To participate in or visit sports events, rehearsals, plays, shows, music programs, cultural activities, museums, etc.

To travel to different parts of the world that we wanted to see and do.

To pursue my academic interests, especially teaching and research—which I was itching to resume (and was missing a lot: "old habits die hard.")

To do volunteer activities, specifically to benefit some of the disadvantaged groups in society.

To read books/articles/periodicals of interest to enrich my mind

To try to supplement "retirement income" because of increased medical expenses and health care costs.

To write books, including this autobiography.

Simply relax, take it easy, and follow a laid-back lifestyle.

Indeed, I could engage in many of these activities simultaneously, although a few required time and concentrated efforts. After a great deal of soul searching and trying to determine priorities, I decided to look for a part-time college teaching opportunity in a neighboring institution. In September 2001, I landed an assignment to teach a course at UMBC in Baltimore. They had a great library and excellent sports facilities that I liked.

Soon the terrorist attacks of 9/11 on New York City's World

Trade Center unfolded. I was horrified to watch the destruction of the Twin Towers. When I went to teach on that day, I choked up in front of the class. I could not talk for several minutes. I stood before the students like a statue! Tears welled up in my eyes. I wanted to share my pain and anguish with my students. They, too, watched me in silence and sadness. Then, after some time, I regained my composure. I told the students how much I loved New York and how my family and friends had spent many happy days walking in the neighborhood of the Twin Towers. I recalled waiting for the super fast elevator to take us to the observation deck of the tower, and the famous World View Restaurant housed in it. I talked about the potential economic magnitude of the destruction brought about by this unprecedented horror, and its psychological impact on the nation. The students listened with rapt attention. I was really moved by their respectful attitude and reaction to my remarks, and my own response to their questions. This was an experience unlike any I had in my teaching career.

The stock market was initially dealt a severe blow by this tragic event. Trading was suspended on the New York Stock Exchange for the next five days. For several months afterward, its negative impact on my retirement portfolio was visible. It took its heavy toll on my finances, until 2003. However, having a few thousand dollars of income (cash flow) from the part-time teaching assignment during those three years helped to cushion the financial blow.

Though I very much enjoyed teaching at UMBC during 2001-'04, it severely restricted my freedom to do other things I wanted to do. The necessity of being in the classroom throughout the academic year (though on a limited basis) pre-empted many other desirable activities. Reluctantly, and after listening to persuasive arguments from Kamala, I decided to quit teaching. Perhaps time will tell if this cessation of academic activity is temporary or permanent.

In the summer of 2002, Kamala's sister Usha came to stay with us for a few months. During the next year, her older sister Prema did likewise. We traveled with them to Alaska and Disneyworld in

179

Florida. I earnestly started working on this autobiography around that time. For intellectual diversion, I got together with some of my friends and started a monthly discussion group. We used to discuss and interchange ideas on many social, economic, moral and philosophical issues. These sessions were very lively and all the participants enjoyed them. Kamala and I also volunteered our services to local charitable causes.

One of the almost unavoidable tasks in retirement is taking care of one's health. In our case, although we try to keep healthy through proper diet and daily exercise, the inevitable ravages of age take their toll. Being diabetic, both Kamala and I need to visit various medical practitioners frequently to deal with different medical problems. The long array of doctor visits, lab tests, eye examinations, dental appointments, physical therapy and other medical chores takes a lot of our time and energy. The associated medical expenses make a significant dent in the family budget. Good health is a great blessing at all times, and especially in our old age. We are truly thankful for whatever benefits we are getting from our retirement medical plan. Without this life support system, it is hard to imagine what living would be like in our golden years.

One always wonders, where does the time go? When you do not have to go to work every day to earn a living, there can be plenty of leisure hours—free time—to do whatever one wants. That is the theory. My actual experience is somewhat mixed. Yes, there is plenty of time available for "non-income-earning activities" one chooses to engage in. But as Parkinson's Law states: "Work expands to fill the available time." This is actually true, even in retirement. That is why, despite all the technological improvements that we have witnessed in recent years (such as computers, cell phones, digital communication systems, microwave ovens and scores of other labor-saving devices we seem unable to live without), people seem to have no time at all. It seems that time has become even more precious and scarce, compared to the years of our youth.

It is now seven years since Kamala and I retired from our jobs. We like our present lifestyle a lot. Being physically near our chil-

180

dren's families is a great boon. We are able to take part in almost all important family functions. We are also able to participate in matters of interest to our neighborhood and community, to enrich our socio-cultural life.

Retirement can be rewarding and enjoyable—but it is hard work!

# Chapter 23

## The River of Life

So far I have been writing about various important events in my life. In describing my life experiences, I was focusing not only on what happened, but also on how and why. I tried to explain how I dealt with many events (not always of my choosing) that happened on the journey, and my reasons for doing so. Wherever possible, I have tried to explain why I did what I did, as well as the rationale behind particular decisions. A sense of control, of being master of one's fate, is absolutely essential if one is to negotiate the journey of life in any meaningful sense. I realize that this is not often possible, especially if external events overwhelm us and submerge our free will. Here and there, I have made some occasional remarks about my attitudes and values. In this chapter, I will try to summarize my philosophy of life and how I formulated those particular values and beliefs that guided me in my decision-making. Hopefully, the interested reader can get some useful insights from these personal reflections.

Life is paradoxical. Here are some examples from my life.

When I was growing up, I often felt hungry, but did not get enough food to satisfy my hunger. Now I have plenty of food available at my disposal and can eat whatever I want, whenever I want; but often I do not feel hungry enough to eat. (Of course I do not have to eat if I don't feel like it—I have the luxury of choice.)

In my youth, I often felt the urge, desire and energy to indulge in many pleasures of the flesh, but on many occasions I did not have the time or the opportunity to do so. Now I have the time, but not the energy or the desire.

There were many times when I wanted to buy something either because I really needed it or thought it would be desirable to have, but lacked the money to buy. Now, even if I have the money, my whole attitude to possessing many material things has changed. I do not feel compelled to buy anything now unless I think it is absolutely essential. I am not interested in the latest gadgets, their "new" and "improved" versions, or the latest fashions. I am quite satisfied to wear the clothes and shoes that I bought a few years back, or drive the ten-year-old car that I still have.

Most of my life, I wanted to win while playing games. Whether I was playing a game of tennis, a chess match or debating some topic with an opponent, winning was the paramount objective. The focus was always on winning. Losing meant defeat and sometimes led even to despondency. This is no longer the case. Nowadays, winning is not much fun unless I am playing against a worthy opponent. Losing with a player better than I is a great deal more satisfying than winning against a weak or unskilled opponent. Winning merely for the sake of winning is no fun at all.

In a sense, the whole of my life has been a battlefield. Many years ago, reading the great Indian epic *Mahabharata* really opened my eyes in a way no other book ever did. The main theme of that great epic is the conflict between evil and good. The so-called evil really is our own base nature (or passions fueled by the ego), personified in the character of individuals such as Duryodhana. On the other hand, the virtues, or good characteristics of human nature, were embodied in the personality of Yudhishtira. Their disparate values, outlook, goals, actions and approach to life's varied challenges made a great impression on me. I learned that many of the problems of living stem from our inability to tame the undesirable elements of our own nature. Understanding their all-powerful grip on our behavior is essential to craft a strategy to deal with them. I therefore tried to develop a philosophy of life around the theme of trying to tame "the seven deadly sins." These are:

Anger, Greed, Envy, Lust, Gluttony, Pride and Sloth.

I have learned that many of the greatest sages, seers and philosophers the world has ever known were sometimes victims of one or the other of these deadly sins (great monsters, as I call them). Various myths and legends were built around the theme of how their inability to subdue these basic passions (or emotions)

184

often led to their ultimate downfall. Many a great hero or heroine of yore, however gifted, powerful or intelligent, was cursed by one of these seven basic weaknesses of human nature. Even some of the all-powerful gods and goddesses were repeatedly tested by these demonic vices.

I have also realized that this universal theme pervaded not only the lives of Indian mythological and historical figures, but also those of other cultures, especially that of ancient Greece. The great Greek heroes and heroines were repeatedly portrayed as pathological victims of these egregious sins. It seemed almost self-evident that human nature was pre-programmed to behave according to the dictates of these pervasive evil influences. There was no escaping from their iron grip on our lives, no matter how hard we tried to shake them off.

It seemed to me that this was a truly formidable challenge worth fighting for. Building one's character and leading an ideal, virtuous life requires confronting these evil proclivities in us with determination and perseverance. I decided to meet the enemy head on. This was going to be a lifelong battle, on a daily basis, until death. Like a valiant Rajput warrior who is prepared to lay down his life to defend his honor and country rather than surrender, I decided to take up arms against these perennial monsters. I knew I needed a strong, steely armor to defend myself. I looked around for the best ones I could find.

Looking through a long list of desirable virtues, I selected seven that I thought were powerful enough to array against the seven deadly vices. Marshalling their aid and heavily fortified, I was ready for battle. I spent a great deal of time and energy in the choice of my defensive armor.

Observing the enemy's powerful and relentless assaults, I concluded that those weapons were very sharp, and could pierce our armor and penetrate our body and mind with deadly force and accuracy. These deadly weapons always hit us with uncanny precision and ferocity. They are relentless in their attack, and our minds are often unable to cope with their superior powers. Therefore, to

185

defend against them needed great care and ingenuity. Protecting against their mighty onslaught required absolute concentration and awareness of their deviousness.

To pursue this battlefield analogy one step further, I was going to pursue a defensive strategy. One cannot destroy these cardinal vices by aggressive behavior, but only by carefully watching their hold on our psyche and protecting against their vicious attack by shaking them off. So, here goes my arsenal of fighting the "war of living honorably":

My armor consists of the following seven cardinal virtues:

Self-control

Discipline

Patience

Contentment

Humility

Forbearance

Will power

I chose self-control as the king of virtues. It is a formidable armor against the onslaught of most of the seven vices. Mastery over our own self is undoubtedly the ultimate guarantee of protection against all evil thoughts and temptations. Self-control is the most difficult virtue to practice. It calls for iron determination and dogged resistance to temptations. Lack of self-control often leads to our downfall in every attack launched by the seven deadly sins. If we are able to practice self-control and use it effectively, the ship of life can navigate through many treacherous, rough waters without getting wrecked on its fateful voyage. Through practicing self-control, we can try to steer ourselves away from being trapped by short-term emotional outbursts of anger or lust that threaten our long-term wellbeing.

Examining the nature of the enemy, it becomes obvious that we often succumb to various temptations because of our desire for immediate pleasure or gratification at the risk of courting their long-term ill effects. It is extremely difficult to resist our desire for quick payoff in our dealings with others. Expressing our anger against someone gives immediate relief from the surging rage. The consequent hurt we impose on others (as well as ourselves, belatedly, through regret) is far from our minds in the heat of the moment. Likewise, eating beyond what the body needs for mere nourishment is extremely enjoyable. Our taste buds cannot resist the urge to fill our bellies with delicious food placed in front of us. The craving for satisfying our palates is irresistible. The ill health caused by this urge to eat or the harm it wreaks on our bodies later does not seem to deter us from our immediate indulgences. Such consequences are not obvious at the moment; their inevitable effects are brushed aside, or seem far in the distant future to worry about.

Reflecting on the adverse consequences of our actions needs mental discipline. To act without thoroughly examining the alternatives available to us is sheer folly. The discipline needed to act rationally and intelligently when confronted with choices in life saves us from unnecessary future regrets. Disciplined behavior paves the way for success and achievement in all walks of life. It protects us from the tyranny of anger, gluttony and lust. To further ensure success in our fight against giving in to their pervasive negative influences, we need to practice patience.

Patience is the exact opposite of an instantaneous, pre-programmed response to provocations. Patience calls for calm reflection. When someone shouts at us angrily, we tend to shout back vigorously, defending our turf. Patience counsels us to reflect before responding thus. It can save us from a lot of later regrets. It is indeed a golden virtue. It commands a premium, almost all the time. Indeed patience can, at times, be far more difficult to practice than the other virtues. It is undoubtedly far easier to succumb to the passions of the moment than to postpone the urge for a quick response. Our minds are preoccupied with short-term or immediate gratification of the senses. Nature has spared little mercy in this respect. Therefore, we need to be ever vigilant and remind ourselves to be patient in those situations where giving in to temptations inevitably leads to subsequent regrets. Our long-term physical and mental wellbeing almost always depends on postponing the urge for immediate gratification of the senses. On these occasions, armed with patience, we can resort to calm reflection, appropriate delayed action and eventual success. One needs to be willing to accept the short-term pain involved in waiting patiently for the sake of obtaining long-lasting benefits. This is of course hard to do, but essential if we are to tame the monster.

Next in my arsenal of the essential virtues comes contentment. To be content with our income, possessions or station in life at a particular time helps to ensure peace of mind. This does not mean giving up the pursuit of whatever it is we want to accomplish. Being content helps me to focus my mind on getting what is important to me, rather than worrying about what others already have. Jealousy is one of the most destructive of human emotions. Unless it is tamed, it constantly poisons our mind and robs us of all mental peace. We become slaves of ever more desires to own and possess what others have, despite the many desirable things we may already have. This tendency of our minds to be perpetually jealous of others can only be overcome by cultivating the habit of contentment. It is the only way to subdue envy and bring sanity to our life. It is an effective antidote to the poisonous influence of the all-powerful weed called envy, which tries to deprive us of mental peace and happiness.

Greed too deprives us of the joy of enjoying whatever we have managed to accumulate. The constant tendency of our minds to want ever-larger quantities of material wealth (or whatever we fancy) can become a curse. It paves the road toward unexpected losses and eventual regret. Excessive greed guarantees the road to unhappiness. The virtue of contentment is therefore an effective remedy against the curse of greediness.

Next in line is the virtue of humility. Excessive pride, egotism and arrogance about one's accomplishments can become the cause of our ultimate downfall. Both material wealth and nonmaterial attributes such as beauty, power, intelligence and education can

188

make us forget our constant need for humility. History is full of examples in which the lack of this great virtue brought about the destruction of many great personalities. Humility helps one to moderate the natural tendency to blow one's own trumpet too loudly, disturbing the tranquility of others. Practicing this golden virtue protects us from unnecessary harm to ourselves and others. The universal tendency to brag about our achievements causes mental distress to others. Humility is the best armor against such pride, i.e., taking ourselves too seriously. It undoubtedly prevents us from ignoring or belittling the successes and virtues of others.

To forbear is to empathize with the weaknesses of other human beings. We grow in strength and stature by forgiving intentional or unintentional harm or hurt caused to us by others. Carrying a grudge against someone for too long a period weakens our own mind and spirit. We rob ourselves of peace of mind and happiness by stressing on the negative rather than the positive aspects of our lives. A great deal of our misery stems from our unwillingness to forgive and forget whatever real or imaginary acts of unkindness life has dealt us in our dealings with others. If the other party is unwilling or unable to correct their lapses, our own willingness to forbear them is the only sensible way to deal with the problem. This act of forbearance then frees us from the clutches the wrong-doer had on our minds.

It seems to me that the strength of our willpower is the ultimate armor against the daily onslaught of every negative trait in human nature. Willpower helps us to withstand the tendency for slothful behavior. Fortunately, we can continue to work at improving our willpower by constant and determined effort. Every little success we have at keeping the seven deadly sins from disturbing our peace of mind should fortify our resolve to keep them at bay. Through repeated practice and perseverance, we can summon the courage to deal with them effectively. This is a lifelong battle, no doubt, but worth fighting for in order to preserve our personal dignity and overall mental equanimity. It may protect us from the tyranny of many unnecessary and avoidable regrets.

This brief foray into a discussion of the seven deadly sins and the seven essential virtues naturally leads to the question: How have I fared?

My own record in dealing with their pervasive influence is somewhat mixed. I have had a few episodes of failure or near failure. Although I have lost some battles, I have had several successes as well. It has been a continuous battle of wits. It is an ongoing, lifelong struggle, sure to continue as long as I live. Every time I win, I am encouraged. Whenever I fail, I redouble my resolve to stand up and fight the next battle. These periodic tests of my willpower have reinforced my resolve to continue to assert my better judgment whenever I am able. There is no doubt that I have learned a great deal about myself through these experiences of self-discovery. When I fail, I do not get discouraged. I tell myself that I will continue my efforts until death.

I am often reminded of the truth of the economist's dictum: As soon as one human "want" is satisfied, another one crops up in its place. We seem to be never satisfied. Many of us are engaged in a perpetual game of seeking new "satisfactions". This seems to be the human condition.

Or is it really? Does it have to be this way? Always? And forever?

Why are we not satisfied with what we already have? Must we keep on hankering after newer and better things all the time? Is this the curse of living? Isn't this constant hankering for more the root of our tensions and headaches? Indeed, isn't it the cause of our perpetual dissatisfaction with modern life, despite all the economic progress and inventions for making life easier, simpler, faster, quicker, ever more convenient?

One epithet says: He who wants nothing has everything. And is, therefore, the richest person in the world!

This is the essence of Buddha's teachings. "Desire leads to suffering. Freeing ourselves from desire leads to Freedom or Nirvana."

Shakespeare said the same thing in his own inimitable words: "Life is a tale, told by an idiot, full of sound and fury, signifying nothing."

Was Shakespeare right?

Throughout my life, I have been searching hard for the meaning of life. And its purpose.

Great philosophers, enlightened seers and wise people have answered this question in different ways. But it seemed to me that no one had a definitive answer yet.

Sometimes I did feel enlightened by them. Or at least I thought so. At other times, I got more confused.

Looking for guidance in the conduct of my life, I sought guidance from various religions. Though their moral and ethical precepts have universal appeal, and they do teach us lessons for the proper conduct of life, we see that there are many contradictions. Conflicts in thinking abound. History shows that religious hatred and intolerance have caused umpteen wars, bitterness and human suffering.

Then I read Bertrand Russell's writings. I liked his sage advice to ignore religions. Religion is not the same as morality or ethics. Nor is it the repository of ultimate or eternal wisdom. But this knowledge was not enough to satisfy me.

I read the Greek philosophers, and the great Greek tragedies. They confused me about their systems of philosophy. There seemed to be no clear direction or instruction about what one should do with one's life.

How should one live?

I sought answers in the great Bhagavad Gita. Lord Krishna counseled three different paths to achieve life's mission. They were:

Knowledge

Devotion to God

Doing one's Duty

All these seemed equally worthwhile. It was up to me to choose.

The same advice was provided in the ancient Upanishads, the repositories of wisdom of the ancient Hindu sages and seers.

Confucius taught me a great deal about how to live.

Although I have not yet read the Bible or the Koran thoroughly, I have perused them. I gained valuable insights from Christ's Golden Rule: "Do unto others as thou would have them do unto you."

Still, I was not satisfied.

I read the great Tamil poet/sage Valluvar's many proverbs. He taught me a great deal. He counseled moderation in everything. "Practice virtuous acts. Always be kind. Don't ever hurt others by uttering unkind words. Words can sometimes hurt more than a knife."

Hurtful words, said in anger, cannot be retrieved. This prescription for rightful living has guided me. Since verbal communication with others takes up most of our life, I have consciously tried to follow this dictum.

Finally, I looked for my answer in a volume on ancient proverbs. Lessons learned from a wide variety of human experiences, distilled from thousands of very wise people throughout the ages, in condensed capsules.

I absorbed what I learned from all these diverse sources into one great thought, which is summarized beautifully in the great Gayathri Mantra:

"Let us Salute the Great Sun who radiates powerful Energy and

Brilliant Light; let us seek Wisdom and Enlightenment as the

Supreme Goals of Life; let our Mind and Spirit meditate with Joy and Strength"

I realized that this is the mantra my grandfather taught me when I was eleven years old, although at that time, I neither under-

192

stood nor paid attention to its profound meaning or significance.

I learned that armed with knowledge, wisdom and discipline, one can achieve almost anything one wants.

It seems to me that our life is like a river flowing. Let me explain.

Every river has a simple beginning. Most of them start from the force of accumulated droplets of rainwater, or perhaps a perennial underground spring.

Human life, too, begins in a similar way.

By the force of gravity, these droplets of water coalesce and form a small stream, brook, rivulet, bayou or run. Call it what you will. They start flowing together with force. This body of water starts gushing downstream. Slowly, they take a distinct shape and form. They grow in size over time and space.

Human life gets its nourishment from the mother's body and starts growing. Every embryo starts this way, taking a distinct shape and personality, and becomes a unique human being.

At first a river is small. It grows bigger and bigger as it flows through the land, accumulating water from its catchment area.

Our bodies too grow in a similar manner. As the years go by, we grow bigger and stronger until we finally reach a certain age.

Depending on the terrain through which it flows, a river cuts deep gorges among highlands and mountains. It winds its way down, no matter how high or low the land through which it flows.

Likewise, nature as well as nurture influences the growth of a human being. We become what we eat; our bodies are big or small, straight or bent, tall or short, depending on several factors.

Some rivers run deep. Others are shallow. Some are treacherous. Others are serene. Some are long. Others are wide. Some rivers can easily be crossed. They are shallow or placid. Others are sometimes unfathomable.

Our personalities, characters, attitudes, interests and abilities differ from one another. Somewhat different from a river, no doubt, but I think there are lots of similarities between the two.

A single river, during its course from its source to its destination, can be turbulent, placid, serene, deep, shallow, straight, winding, sometimes dry or at other times overflowing its banks. In a similar fashion, a human being can be subject to varied states of minds, moods, emotions and changing physical conditions.

During their course downstream, many great rivers are fed by innumerable other streams. Sometimes there are many small and large tributaries. So the original river can get very, very big. Like the Missouri-Mississippi. Or the Amazon. Or many other great rivers of the world.

In a way, human life, too, undergoes a similar transformation. We get married. We have children. And grandchildren. And great, great, grandchildren. We acquire many other relatives, too. Our families grow bigger and bigger over time. And I include friends, too, in this analogy.

We always say: Our family and friends, our community, our relationships with other human beings make us who we are and what we become.

Sometimes a river has moods. Depending on the season, it can become nasty or treacherous. It can overflow its bounds. It gets bloated. It can cause huge floods, but sometimes it shrinks in size as well, and causes draught in the land it flows through. Many rivers, like the Yellow River in China, are known for the terrible floods and destruction they cause. They destroy, just as they create and nourish life.

Are human beings any different? They too can put on weight, get bloated. They can go on a diet, lose weight and shrink in size. They too can create and destroy. They can bestow great good, or cause immense harm on other human beings.

Rivers nourish us and sustain life, much more than they destroy. Most of the rivers in the world since ancient times have sustained every civilization known to man. Every city in the ancient

194

world was built near a river. This ensured availability of water and the city's survival. If the river moved (as they sometimes did, changing their course) the city too had to move along with it.

Is our species any different? We may stay put, or move, or migrate, or rebuild.

A river's course can only move forward, never backward. Its inexorable progress toward the sea ends its mission. It has served its purpose when it ultimately joins the sea.

Human life too only moves forward. We cannot go backward in time. Our life, after its purpose has been served, ends with death.

It seems to me that there is an uncanny similarity between rivers and humans. Both are products of nature. Both are subject to its inexorable laws. Sometimes both are unpredictable. Most of the time, both of them are benevolent and do more good than harm. They both need nourishment (water) for their survival.

Of course this similarity has its limitations. Unlike humans, rivers cannot think. They have no memory. They cannot reproduce themselves.

Rivers have held a fascination for me all my life. One of my favorite pastimes since childhood has been to study the world atlas, looking at the courses of the great rivers. I have read with delight several articles in *National Geographic* describing the Amazon, the Nile, the Congo, the Ganges, the Euphrates, and the Danube, the Volga and the Yangtze. Whenever I see a small stream flowing along the road on which I am driving, I am fascinated by its ebb and flow. Many times, I have stopped my car, gotten down, and sat on the banks of the river and enjoyed looking at the water for hours. It gives me serenity and peace of mind. The rhythm of the river is so soothing to our senses. It helps to clear the mind. To me, it is one of the great joys of living.

I had a great spiritual experience when I stood under the great Niagara Falls (on the Buffalo, New York, side of the river). On previous visits to see the Falls, I had always stayed on the Canadian side. During my most recent visit a few years back, I stayed

195

on the American side for the first time. Along with family members visiting from India, I climbed down the long, winding path leading up to the Falls. Finally, I was standing directly under the torrential cascade of water streaming down like an avalanche. I lifted my face, wondering at this supreme power of nature. It was awesome to behold.

I was humbled by its majesty and grandeur. I then felt an absolute sense of peace and supreme joy. It was an experience filled with pure ecstasy. I felt a sense of awe and wonder. It was a feeling of being uplifted toward heaven. This kind of indescribable feeling I had never experienced before. It was a spiritual awakening for me. I saw the great beauty of nature at its best. The feeling of oneness with nature was utterly uplifting. I also experienced a sense of wonder and bewilderment that was truly one of a kind. I thanked the almighty (power of nature) for this wonderful experience.

The Niagara Falls, born of a river, gave me a unique gift. Not merely seeing one of the great wonders of nature, but to become one with nature.

# Chapter 24

## Some Nuggets of Wisdom

Life has taught me a lot. I owe a great deal of what I have learned to my teachers. I had the good fortune to interact with many learned scholars. Many books on philosophy and ethics have shaped my innermost thoughts. Several memorable personal experiences, both pleasant and unpleasant, have also contributed to my outlook on life. In addition, a lot of reflection and the habit of constantly examining my life have provided some valuable insights. What follows in this chapter are culled from what I have read, discussed, experienced and mulled over for many years. They are the essence of what I have learned about life. I offer it to the reader as a gift.

A few years ago, I read in the *New York Times* a beautiful story about a young man from a very poor family growing up to become the valedictorian of his high school graduating class. He had literally "pulled himself up with his bootstraps." His speech to his classmates ended with the following words:

"Life is a book. You are the author. Write a beautiful story."

I was moved by this message. It had universal appeal, and it touched me deeply.

During one of the 1979 election debates between President Jimmy Carter and the then presidential candidate Ronald Reagan, the defining question put before the voters was:

"Are you better off now than you were four years ago?"

It seemed to me that this was a profound question about perspective. Reagan asked the voters to evaluate Mr. Carter's presidency in a nutshell. In doing so, he had hit upon the proverbial nail.

In evaluating my own life, I am confronted with the same kind

197

of question:

"Am I better off now than I was forty or so years ago?" Before I came to America?

In order to answer this question truthfully, one has to define what "better off" really means.

Surely, life is multi-dimensional. One can be better off in some ways and worse off in other ways. It is almost impossible to say that one is better off in every respect, compared with living in another time and place.

When I left India in 1963, the rupee/dollar exchange rate was about Rs.4.86 to $1. In 2007, the exchange rate is roughly Rs.44.52 to $1. During these forty-four years, the Indian rupee has depreciated about tenfold. In very rough terms, the purchasing power of the rupee is now about 10 percent of what it used to be four decades earlier. This is by no means an exact comparison, but it gives a reasonable approximation of the rate of inflation that has taken place in India during these four decades.

Measured in this way, some of the income figures I mentioned earlier in this book are highly distorted. They ought to be increased at least tenfold to make a meaningful comparison (in terms of purchasing power). Even such an adjustment would be really arbitrary. Many, indeed most, of the goods and services that enter into the average Indian family's consumption basket are domestically produced. Because of differences in climate, culture and ways of living, it is not possible to make a fair comparison of what a dollar buys in America with what it can buy in India. Internationally traded goods and services, especially manufactured goods, have roughly similar price structures in both countries. But most non-traded goods and services (which really matter for this comparison) have very dissimilar price structures. Therefore, the internal purchasing power of the rupee is very different from its international exchange value.

There is no doubt that I am economically much better off today than I was in India. My present standard of living in America (as well as the lifestyle to which I have become accustomed) is much better than what it used to be. There is absolutely no question about this. "How much better?" is impossible to say. Nor is it really necessary. Therefore, in my case, the answer to Mr. Reagan's question is a resounding "YES" from a purely economic perspective.

Not only this. As an Indian immigrant, I have been able to help various family members in India financially for over forty years. Such help would have been impossible had I stayed in India. There is no doubt that they are better off, thanks to the monetary payments they received. Had I stayed and worked in India all my life, this important monetary contribution to their economic wellbeing would have been absent, or limited at best.

Almost everything in life is relative. There are probably no absolute measures or standards by which we can judge, or measure, one situation from another. We all get used to what we have, and continue to hanker after what we do not have.

"The pursuit of happiness" is one part of the well-known human "Bill of Rights" enshrined in the American Constitution. The founding fathers thought it fit to include this as one of our fundamental rights, along with life and liberty.

What constitutes happiness? This is a wide-open question, with no easy answer. The term "happiness" is hard to define precisely. However, there is generally wide agreement among philosophers that "a sense of overall wellbeing and satisfaction with one's station in life" is an important ingredient of a happy state of mind.

This may include, among other things: health, wealth, a meaningful job, one's cherished achievements, love, family, freedom (political as well as religious) and probably wisdom.

The list could be endless. But no single item is absolutely essential to be happy. And people who have all these things (and a lot more besides) may not be necessarily happy.

Philosophers and thinkers have debated this question since the beginning of time. Many people in poor countries are (or seem to be) happy, despite their poverty. People who are not healthy are not necessarily unhappy on that account alone. Unemployed people are not necessarily unhappy, nor does having a good (meaningful) job ensure happiness. Indeed, many other ingredients of happiness that I listed, such as achievement, love, family and freedom, are not always sufficient to promote happiness in everybody.

Beautiful people are not any happier than "plain" ones. Powerful individuals are not, either. Even wisdom does not always guarantee a happy state of mind.

So, we come back to the basic question: What is happiness? How can one be happy?

My conclusion, after a lot of study, observation and personal experience, is that "happiness is a state of not wanting anything other than what one already has."

This very loose and admittedly broad statement is the best one I can muster with regard to what it means to be happy. If this is accepted, then as long as we do not feel deprived by the absence of something we do not already have—whether it be money, job, love, possessions, power, knowledge, health, achievements or whatever—we can be said to be happy.

Here I am obviously referring to both material and non-material aspirations in life. Probably this is why the founding fathers used the words "pursuit of happiness." We constantly "pursue" happiness, chasing it, as it were. Happiness is elusive. The pursuit of it is endless, and perhaps frustrating. However, we seem to be preoccupied with it, all the time.

The reason for this perpetual hunt is obvious. Without having in our possession what we are currently seeking, we seem to be unhappy. We think we would attain a true state of happiness if and when we get what we want, and seek. As soon as we get it, we do feel happy, for a while at least. But the novelty soon wears off. Having achieved what we were seeking, it no longer seems to ensure a continued state of happiness. Something else (a new want, or aspiration to have something else) takes its place, with the obvi-

200

ous need to chase this new goal.

This pursuit, this perpetual game of chicken, goes on endlessly, continuously, and forever, until we are satiated with everything we think we want. Of course this is a never-ending, lifelong phenomenon.

Many of us also seem to want what someone already possesses. We may not have really thought about it earlier. Not having it previously did not cause any problem or unhappiness, until we encounter it anew. But now, having seen what the other person already has, we too seem to want that. Somehow, in our mind, what we do not have seems to be more desirable or valuable than what we already possess. If what we possess is snatched away from us, we feel miserable. Being deprived of it makes us very unhappy, indeed. Then, to restore our previous state of equanimity, we want to repossess what we have just lost. In fact, as psychologists have warned us, losses (things taken away from us) can be much more painful than gains of a comparable amount.

Now, with this analysis of what makes us happy or unhappy, at last I am able to evaluate my own life. Applying the principles I just stated, I sought certain goals in life, and succeeded in achieving most of them. That certainly made me happy, for a while. Not achieving those goals would have made me miserable, no doubt.

While pursuing those goals, I sometimes used to wonder whether the benefits were worth the costs. The struggles, frustrations, disappointments, setbacks, pain and suffering I endured (while chasing my goals) were very real. Experiencing those negative feelings made me very uncomfortable at that time. Nevertheless, I persisted in the pursuit of my goals because I thought that eventual success would guarantee my happiness. And indeed, it did, for a while. Each time I got what I wanted, I felt happy and fulfilled.

In retrospect, I think the eventual benefits of those pursuits were perhaps worth the costs. I say "perhaps" because I am not absolutely sure about this. I will probably never know. Probably this is how life is lived by every one of us. Throughout our lives,

201

each one of us strives to reach some goal, short term or long term, material or spiritual, temporary or permanent. This is what "living" entails. Without such striving and constant activity to engage our faculties, life would not be worth living. We would be bored to death. Again, all these things differ from person to person. Ultimately, it all depends on what we want from living our life.

One of the frequent questions sometimes asked by reporters is, "If you had to live your life again, would you have done it differently?"

It is an interesting question, but really difficult to answer. It assumes that one can be selective in choosing to undo certain things that we did in our life earlier. Perfect knowledge about the outcome of our decisions is impossible. The future cannot be predicted with certainty. If we knew that the choices we made in a certain situation (in the past) would lead to undesirable/unwanted results, we might not have made those choices in the first place. Everyone hopes that the choices they do make turn out to be the right ones. It is impossible to always choose those alternatives that lead to success, and avoid those that end in failure.

Therefore, even if we could have made a different choice in those cases where the outcomes turned out to be bad, we could not always avoid making some "bad" decisions. Turning some failures into successes would probably imply turning other successes into failures. The consequent minuses would probably cancel out the pluses, leaving the overall lifetime balance sheet not materially different from the original one.

If I knew then what I know now, I certainly would not have made some of the choices I did make. Complete knowledge and perfect wisdom would have turned me into a God (assuming God is perfect and knows everything perfectly). But humans are fallible; there is no escaping from this truth. All we can hope for is to minimize the mistakes we make, and maximize the "satisfactions" we get, through constant learning and practice.

This realization leads me to summarize what I have learned.

It is better to earn more money and pay more taxes (and/or help society in many other ways) than to earn less and help others less.

But merely having more money does not guarantee a better life, or more happiness.

Greater income and wealth increases our ability to help others. This increases our satisfaction from living.

Life is a one-way journey; therefore, one should try to appreciate the scenery while it lasts.

Being able to help others in whatever way we can, whenever we can, increases the sum of human wellbeing.

You don't miss what you don't know, or what you don't want, however pleasurable the experience of having it may be to others.

It is a truism that spending money is easy, while saving it is difficult, just as putting on weight is easy, but losing that weight is much harder. This is because most indulgences are more pleasurable and easier than acts of self-denial, discipline and self-control. But a time comes in almost everyone's life when the accumulated costs of our past indulgences far exceed their short-term benefits. Therefore, wisdom counsels us to deny ourselves some short-term pleasures (or practice self-restraint) for the sake of our longer term, overall wellbeing.

A positive attitude, appropriate discipline and strong willpower are far more important than anything else in our journey through life.

We have to deal with reality: "what is," not "what might have been." To paraphrase Abraham Lincoln: "If wishes were horses, beggars would ride them." Wishing problems away does not make them disappear. We have to deal with them throughout life as best as we can.

Just because something is good for my neighbor, does not mean it is necessarily good for me.

We cannot easily return to where we came from; too many changes have taken place there, as well as in ourselves. We become misfits in our old roles. So we have to adjust and adapt constantly to suit new conditions and circumstances.

Some things are hard to learn and do, no matter how sincerely we try. Everyone cannot do everything, no matter how easy it is for others. Even trying to do some things may not be worth the effort. So, let me do what I can do, and leave others to do what I cannot do at all.

No matter how tasty and good the food is, if you cannot eat it, money spent on it is wasted.

Many proverbs have a lot of wisdom and experience packed into them, but they are not always helpful to everyone and everybody. And some of them are downright irrelevant. We should choose them carefully before applying them to ourselves.

We can put off some unpleasant problems until we are ready to deal with them; but sooner or later, one day, they become an urgent reality, and then we are forced to take action. The day of reckoning always arrives, sometimes belatedly.

Character is the most important asset one can have. It takes a long time to build, and requires great effort to maintain, but it can be destroyed by a single act of poor judgment. It is like a tree that takes years to grow but can be brought down in an instant. We should be constantly vigilant to safeguard our character.

Learning never stops. Knowledge is power. And it is a great asset that can be used to our advantage, almost always.

Having a sense of control over our life is far more important than anything else I can think of.

All of us need a definite goal, a purpose in life, to make it tolerable as well as enjoyable.

Things worth doing are not always worth doing well. We should try to do our best, and leave it there, even if the result is not perfect. Perfection is not worth pursuing. The cost is incredibly high.

Our ancestors knew far more than we sometimes give them

credit for.

Most of us seem to be bent on focusing our energies on what we don't have rather than on what we do have. Often, we take our successes for granted, and bemoan our failures. This is a definite waste of time and energy. It diminishes our enjoyment of living.

Robert Louis Stevenson wrote: "It is better to travel than to arrive." He certainly knew what he was talking about. We should enjoy the journey—that is what is important, not the destination.

I have almost finished what I wanted to say. One concluding thought, and it summarizes the essence of everything I have learned.

Our beliefs drive our lifelong decisions. They have great power over the choices we make. We have the freedom to believe anything we want. What we believe may not necessarily be true. Similarly, just because we refuse to believe in something does not make it untrue or wrong. Therefore, we must choose our beliefs very carefully; examine them periodically; and be prepared to reevaluate them constantly. Since our actions are driven by our belief system, this process helps to ensure that we do what is right. We are, or may ultimately become, what we believe. Hence, to gain control of our own lives, we must be selective in choosing what we believe. This, I have learned, is the recipe for the good life.

**THE END**